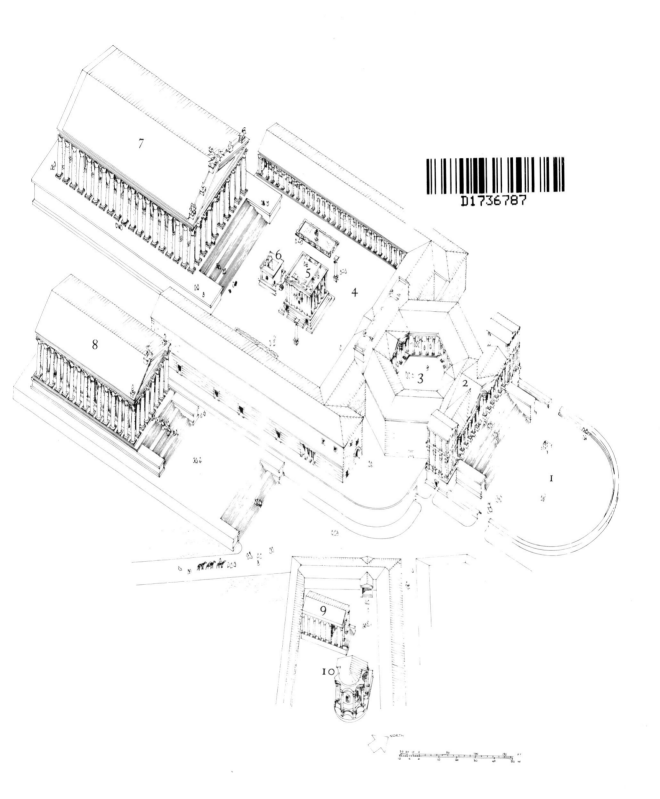

NORTH

CO3286789

BAALBEK

BAALBEK

by

FRIEDRICH RAGETTE

With an Introduction by
Sir Mortimer Wheeler

Noyes Press

Copyright © 1980 by Friedrich Ragette
Library of Congress Catalog Card Number: 80-19626
ISBN: 0-8155-5059-6
Printed in Great Britain

Published in the United States by
NOYES PRESS
Noyes Building
Park Ridge, New Jersey 07656

Library of Congress Cataloging in Publication Data

Ragette, Friedrich.
  Baalbek.

  Bibliography: p.
  Includes index.
  1. Baalbek—History. 2. Architecture, Roman—
Lebanon—Baalbek. I. Title.
DS89.B3R33   939'.44   80-19626
ISBN 0-8155-5059-6

CONTENTS

CONTENTS

PICTURE SOURCES

The illustrations on the front endpapers and those on pages 28, 29, 31, 36, 70, 77, 103, 104, 118 & 119 are by the author. Neil Hyslop drew the maps on pages 12 and 64 as well as the back endpapers. Photographs reproduced by courtesy of the National Council of Tourism in Lebanon appear on pages 17 (photo Yetenegian), 25, 26, 36, 38 (photo Magnin), 45, 46 (photo Magnin), 48, 112 (photo Fattal) and 113 (photo Manoug). The photograph on page 21 was supplied by the Réunion des musées nationaux, Paris, that on page 67 by the Beirut National Museum, and that on page 114 by Mr Randle.

The remaining illustrations, from published sources, are taken from the three volumes of Theodor Wiegand's *Baalbek* with the following exceptions: page 35 from Collart & Coupel; p. 52, Cassas; pp. 54 & 80 (photos RIBA) and 88–9, Wood; p. 86, Maundrell (photo RIBA); p. 93 and p. 120 (photo RIBA), Roberts. Complete reference to the works of these authors may be found in the bibliography. The illustrations on p. 60 are from Kähler, *Hadrian und seine Villa bei Tivoli* (Berlin, 1950) and, right, Köpf, *Baukunst in fünf Jahrtausenden* (Stuttgart, 1960); on p. 115 from von Klinckowstroem, *Geschichte der Technik* (Munich, 1959); on p. 117 from Alberti, *Ten Books on Architecture* (London, 1955); and on p. 118 from Fontana, *Castelli e Ponti di Maestro Niccolo Zabaglia* (Rome, 1743).

INTRODUCTION

Size and Baalbek

by Sir Mortimer Wheeler

On a warm day of summer, the notes on which the following reflections are based were scribbled in the expansive shadows of the temple-ruins at Baalbek, in Lebanon. These temples have been familiar since their admirable publication by Robert Wood in 1757, but they have never before received the full analytical appreciation which is their due.*

It is not growing like a tree. . . . The poet wrote of Man, and Man as the ultimate standard of all size need not, outside a company of Footguards, regard the trivial vacillation of his inches. In other manifestations, Size is a matter of moment. Look at a Little Pyramid; a Big Pyramid has to fight hard enough for intelligent recognition, but those *little* pyramids that the Pharaonic builders did not hesitate to scatter round and about are surely silly toys beyond belief. And imagine a *little* Empire State Building, bereft of the size and vista that give some sort of status, I suppose, to the actual pile; the thought horrifies. Imagine a *little* St. Peter's, such as can in fact be seen somewhere in Canada, lacking altogether that superhuman, super-personal, immensity that in Rome at once conditions the mind to all measure of other-worldly emotion. Size.

'We shall realize that size', says Julian Huxley, 'which we are so apt to take for granted, is one of the most serious problems with which evolving life has had to cope. . . . Simply magnify an object without changing its shape and, without meaning to, you have changed all its properties'. And not only is this true of evolving life; it is equally true of evolving art and architecture, if indeed these be other than forms of evolving life. For instance, the crowning gift of the Roman Empire to architecture was magnitude. With magnitude of course went many other qualities, but most of them were in some measure attendant upon magnitude; they were the changing 'properties' which magnitude implied and begat. And they were literally of epoch-making importance. Those, if such there be, who still regard Roman architecture as a sort of rubiginous autumn phase of the Hellenic tradition may pause and think for a moment in the light of the biological analogue.

* 'Size and Baalbek' was first published in *Antiquity*, Vol XXXVI, 1962. Sir Mortimer Wheeler kindly allowed it to be reprinted as the Introduction to this book after receiving a copy of Dr. Ragette's text. He also generously agreed, shortly before his death, to a small but significant alteration in the second sentence of the preamble, the word 'before' being substituted for 'perhaps' which appeared in the original version.

PUBLISHER'S NOTE

BAALBEK

The great buildings of the Roman Empire were *large* buildings. The 'little' temple on the so-called acropolis of Roman Baalbek is bigger than the Parthenon. But let us begin with the Parthenon and its kin.

On the Acropolis of Athens in the latter half of the 5th century B.C. the Greeks said practically all that they had to say about architecture. To the Doric Parthenon, the Ionic Erechtheum and temple of Athena Nike, the Doric and Ionic Propylaea, all between 447 and 405 B.C. – how short a space! – to these one further achievement must be added: the invention of the Corinthian capital at Bassae, far off in the Peloponnese. But that too was contrived by or under the principal architect of the Parthenon within the same time-span. In more than one respect the temple at Bassae was a lonely and precocious work of genius, of which a word later. Meanwhile, a firm line may be drawn across the history of European architecture in 400 B.C. The next phase of active evolution began more than four centuries later; before turning to that let us glance briefly at the architectural legacy of Periclean Greece.

The first point about Hellenic architecture is that it is essentially extrovert. The Parthenon is probably the most intelligent extrovert building that the world has seen. True, it imprisoned in its crepuscular interior the massive gold-and-ivory bulk of Athena, just as it imprisoned the more secular tribute of the faithful; it was a religious safe-deposit. But to the world it showed a plain and sturdy exterior set squarely and possessively on its rock and owing its sturdiness to infinite judgment and finesse. It showed too an impersonal pageant of heroic but utterly extrovert mimes, impeccably wrought, chiselled (at their best) as marble may never be chiselled again, but with nothing whatever in their heads. Neither the building nor its decoration had any inner life; it was a perfect exterior, a perfect piece of man-made geology, and *because* it was, within its proper limitations, perfect it marks an end. The finality of the Parthenon, architecturally and sculpturally, is its defining quality.

I referred just now to the temple at Bassae, and do so again for good reason. It was built perhaps only a dozen years after the Parthenon, but already it holds the seeds of new growth. Its first use of the Corinthian capital has already been recalled. It was also the first classical temple to have an *inside* as well as an outside. For one reason or another, its sculptural frieze was carried round *inside*, not as on the Parthenon outside, the cella or shrine. This was an anticipatory change of great interest. It was still-born; the seeds of new ideas fall often enough on unfructuous ground long before they find a soil in which they can germinate. The arch and the vault provide an example of this; the Greeks knew the principles of both, but left it almost entirely to the Etruscans and the Romans to make free and explicit use of them. So at Bassae we have a desolate and untimely pioneer of the rich Order and the rich interior that were between them to dominate the architecture of the Roman Empire: an architecture that was to look more and more inward, to become more and more – in a crude usage of the term – introvert.

For the Roman problem was above all to create and adorn *interiors*, larger and more magnificent interiors to match imperial pride and the growing self-consciousness and importance of the individual. Here I am not concerned with the multiple social, economic and aesthetic origins of this new phase, springing as they did from a world which spanned south-eastern Europe and western Asia. Still less need I argue again its technical aspects, such as the increasing exploitation of 'concrete' from the 2nd century B.C. onwards. By the end of the 1st century A.D. the whole complex process was in its early prime. It had indeed become inevitable from the time of Alexander the Great, who was of course the real founder of the Roman Empire.

The earliest surviving triumph of this revolution is Hadrian's Pantheon. Its scarified exterior was ever a poor, mean thing. Its interior, lightened by its wall-recesses and strong in the powerful lines of its superbly coffered dome, is one of man's rare masterpieces. There is surely no grander building in the world. They were right to bury Raphael within it.

Now what has happened in the five-and-a-half centuries between the Parthenon and the Pantheon? Bluntly, architecture has been turned outside-in. The mind of man has itself been turned outside-in. Philosophy and religion have combined to alter the shape of the world and man's relationship with it. That world has ceased to be a collection of disjected phenomena, expressed politically by a scatter of city-states; it has become a coherent cosmos, expressed politically by an empire. Its encompassing vault finds a proper symbol in the Pantheon, which stands for Rome just as the objective Parthenon, perched on its Acropolis like a (very distinguished) ornament upon a mantelpiece, stands for Hellas.

'My intention had been that this sanctuary of All Gods should reproduce the likeness of the terrestrial globe and of the stellar sphere, that globe wherein are enclosed the seeds of eternal fire, that hollow sphere containing all'. That is Hadrian speaking of his Pantheon; he is using the words of Mme. Yourcenar, but it is the authentic voice. It is the voice of the cosmos, but it is also Hadrian's. And that is of course the nub of the matter. To vary the picture, the Roman Empire was in large measure monolithic; it was a monarchy; its ultimate doctrine was monotheism. But, of no less importance, its monarch was, for good or ill, an intensely human individual, and it discovered its crowning god in a Man.

So in a fashion, and a significant one, our journey from the Parthenon to the Pantheon has taken us from the pageant to the personality. Strangely enough, yet quite rationally, the growth and the growing coherence of the civilized world has found a counterpart in the growing importance of the individual. And that – to revert – is why the insides of buildings are now so important. The individual devotee goes *inside* his mithraeum or his chapel for personal interchange with his deity; and, where old extrovert temples were used for this purpose, the open colonnades were now walled up, as in the cathedral church (ex-temple of Athena) at Syracuse, or formerly in the Parthenon itself; to ensure privacy within for the mysteries of the initiate. The temples were literally turned outside-in.

But I began with Magnitude, and with Magnitude I want to end. Here, alongside godliness, we have to deal with cleanliness – surely a tolerably in-dividual virtue. It has long been an axiom of architectural history that the great public bath-buildings which constituted the social rendezvous of the Roman world were a leading stimulus in the development of spacious and ornate interiors. You went to the baths in great numbers to talk to and about your friends and to work off the night-before. But one thing you certainly did not do; you never glanced at the untidy complex of domes and gables outside as you entered. (For a small example, look at the confusedly functional exterior of the substantially complete 'Hunting Baths' at Leptis Magna.) It was the inside of the building that mattered, with its towering wall-spaces that stretched the minds of architect and sculptor and gave a sense of self-importance and well-being to patron or client. The great hall of the Baths of Diocletian, enshrined by Michelangelo and Vanvitelli in Santa Maria degli Angeli, is sufficient witness.

With these mountainous structures I am not now concerned. Their magni-tude and character depended from the use of vast concrete vaults and domes. But these present scraps are scribbled in the shadow of Roman vastness of a dif-ferent though allied sort. The temples of Baalbek owe nothing of their quality to such new-fangled aids as concrete. They stand passively upon the largest hewn stones in the world, and some of their columns are the tallest from anti-quity. There were once others at Cyzicus in the north which beat them by an inch or two, but Cyzicus is in limbo. Here at Baalbek we have the last great monument in the outworn trabeate tradition of the Hellenic world. And yet how new it is.

It is new for the reason which we have already discussed. It is new because of its magnitude and of the challenge which magnitude has thrown to the archi-tect. Save for the stupendous podium and half-a-dozen bare pillars, the mighty temple of Jupiter has vanished; but its generous forecourt remains, with some of its detail, to be seen either on the spot or in the gracious and precious engravings issued long ago by the adventurous Robert Wood. And a few yards away stands, still in miraculous perfection, the large but lesser temple, so-called of Bacchus (? Venus), which is a carved jewel. The whole group belongs to the latter half of the 2nd century A.D. and the beginning of the 3rd.

And see what the architect has done with these great wall-spaces. Look first at the 'Bacchus' temple: its interior a riot of ornament within controlling verti-cal and horizontal lines; its slender Corinthian columns carried up to an en-crusted architrave, through two stages of niches with semicircular and pedi-mental heads, frames for vanished statuary; its dramatic daïs on which stood the figure of the deity beneath a baldachin that was certainly of an equal splen-dour. Look too at the *quality* of all this finery, its superb carving, and the sensibility with which it is gently disciplined by the rigid frames and flutings. Here again is a masterpiece, using no structural device unknown to the builders of the Parthenon but attempting and achieving something fresh. It is the *interior* of this building that is its purposed climax, just as, a few decades earlier, it was the *interior* of the Pantheon that mattered.

So too the walls of the Great Court in front of the Jupiter temple, with their rounded and angular alcoves, their double tier of round-headed or pedimental recesses, some with shell-hoods, and their ordered lines of columns. This is not decadence, it is prophecy. It all looks forward with direct prevision to the world of Palladio and his successors; to country-houses of the 18th century English countryside; to the age of elegance that preceded the industrial revolution with its instinctive reversion to muscular Doric or romantic, escapist Gothic.

Nor may I omit the little rotund temple so-called of 'Venus' outside the main group; it was known to Borromini and has been recognized as the prototype of the lantern above the dome of his chapel of S. Ivo (*c.* 1650) in Rome.

Baalbek is the end of one tradition and the beginning of another. Meanwhile it fitted the temper of the world into which it was born. It represents that momentary pause, which might properly be called the 'Antonine pause', in an age of vital transmutation; that moment of balance that was 'the period in the history of the world during which the condition of the human race was most happy and prosperous'. In so doing, and in its own right, Baalbek remains one of the very great monuments in the history of European architecture; a position for which geographically it only just qualifies, for beyond the hills of Anti-Lebanon which rise above it to the east begin the sands of Asia and an essentially alien mind.

CHAPTER ONE

The Site

I T is a drive through countryside of great scenic beauty which brings the visitor of today from Beirut to Baalbek. The busy modern road climbs swiftly up the densely populated western slopes of the Lebanon range, offering lovely glimpses back at the Lebanese capital jutting out into the dark blue Mediterranean. The road reaches its highest point among barren surroundings on the Dahr el Baidar pass at an altitude of 1556 m (5100 ft) and descends steeply into territory that seems arid and empty. As the first view of the broad Beqa'a valley below opens up, the traveller is taken completely by surprise.

This fertile valley looks rather like a richly coloured plain. The Litani river flowing to the south cannot be seen, because its stream is spread over the whole area in a maze of irrigation channels. Before it was irrigated and drained the plain had numerous swampy spots; hence the Arabic name *Biqa'*, the plural of *Buq'ah*, meaning a place with stagnant water. It is Lebanon's only significant agricultural area – about 175 km (110 miles) in length, 10 to 16 km (6 to 10 miles) in width – and it stretches in a north–south direction between the Lebanon and Anti-Lebanon mountain ranges. Joshua called it the 'Valley of Lebanon', and the classical writers referred to it as Coele-Syria (hollow Syria) and one of the 'Granaries of Rome'.

The valley ends in the south with the artificial lake of Karaoun, where the waters of the Litani are collected together before they drop down to a power station and are diverted to new irrigation areas. But the depression extends even further south through the Houli marshlands to lake Tiberias, the river Jordan and the Dead Sea.

Surprisingly, the Beqa'a valley also descends at its northern end, giving birth to the El-A'asi river and merging with the plains of Homs. *El-A'asi* means 'the rebel' in Arabic, because it is the only river between the Mediterranean and the Arabian Gulf which flows in a northward direction. The altitude of the valley averages between 900 and 1000 m (3000 to 3300 ft). Descending from Dahr el Baidar we reach the plain at Chtaura. The road now proceeds northward past fields and vineyards, the land growing less fertile as it gradually rises to its highest level at the watershed between the two rivers. It is here at 85 km (53 miles) from Beirut that we reach our destination: Baalbek.

Being at a level of about 1150 m (3800 ft), the impression is still of a continuous plain. In fact, the watershed is so gradual that it is not certain whether the waters from the spring of Ras el Ain to the south east of Baalbek and from the spring of Ain Lejouj some 8 km east of the town become part of the northward flowing Orontes (El-A'asi) or the southward flowing Leontes

(Litani). These springs have always been the economic basis of the town. Their sparkling water flows quietly past the houses and is then distributed in the fields to the west, where there are abundant groves of apricots, walnuts, grapes and mulberry trees. Large groups of silver poplar provide wood for construction, and, wherever there is irrigation, beans, corn and wheat are also grown. The lush green of the plantations contrasts sharply with the barren reddish slopes of the distant mountains, some of which carry glistening patches of snow for most of the year. Their soft solemn mass streaked with deep purple shadows appears to be lower than its true height of more than 3000 m (9900 ft), that is 2000 m (6600 ft) above the plain. The city is blessed with a bracing climate, and the whole environment must have been really wonderful before the deplorable deforestation of the mountains took place. Tacitus tells us that in his time the summits of Lebanon were still shaded with trees.

The area of Baalbek and particularly the Hermel district to the north of it are among the least westernized parts of Lebanon. We find large numbers of mudbrick houses with internal courtyards which are typical of the desert region to the east. Nomadic tribes with camel caravans regularly move into the plain and pitch their black tents. In the few scattered villages tribalism is still strong and family feuds abound. The growing of hashish is quite common in the area, and the barren mountain vastness is a haven for fugitives from justice.

Today Baalbek is a district capital with about 15 000 inhabitants, mainly farmers, merchants and government employees. Two-thirds of them are Muslims. There are six mosques, three churches and twelve schools, a Palestinian refugee camp and three cinemas.

Although Baalbek is without question the foremost tourist site in Lebanon, it has only two hotels: the Palmyra, officially rated as first class, and the second class Khawam Palace. The reason is that for most tourists Baalbek is a day's excursion from Beirut. Were it not for the magnificent archaeological remains, the town would be of purely local importance today.

CHAPTER TWO

Early History

EARLY in the twelfth century B.C. a horde of people overran Palestine and was only with difficulty prevented from entering Egypt by Rameses III, first pharaoh of the twentieth dynasty. These 'sea peoples', as they were called by the Egyptians, settled in coastal Palestine, eventually merging with the local Canaanites. They were mostly Achaean Greeks who had been expelled from the Aegean Islands by the invading Dorian Greeks. The Canaanites called the sea peoples Philistines, from which the term Palestine is derived, while the term Phoenicians, from Greek *phoinix*, meaning purple-red, was applied by the Hellenic Greeks to the coastal dwellers, who were famous for their purple dye industry.

From Egyptian sources we learn of the naval power of the Achaeans, which was instrumental in giving naval superiority to the Phoenicians, who soon dominated Mediterranean trade from their city states of Sidon, Tyre and Byblos.

This coincided with the domestication of the camel, which introduced caravan trade between Mesopotamia and the Phoenician coast of the Mediterranean via the desert. Thus the cities of Phoenicia became the harbours closest to the goods of the East. Previous and subsequent travellers or conquerors who did not rely on the camel were obliged to make the detour through the northern part of the Fertile Crescent.

For the traders who took this short-cut through the immense Mesopotamian plain, the mountains of the Lebanon range were the last physical obstacle on their way to the sea. To reach the rich, coastal cities of the Phoenicians, where the goods of the East were received for shipment across the Mediterranean, the caravans had a choice of many routes over a variety of passes. The shortest and best route was that which led across the main Lebanon range directly to the coastal destination, be it Sidon, Byblos or Tyre. To move along the coast was impractical for both political and topographical reasons: the chain of city-states was in a constant state of rivalry, and there were numerous rivers to be forded and rugged promontories to be cleared. It was much easier to follow the eastern slopes of the coastal range through the wide and fertile valley known as the Beqa'a. The caravans entered this artery and from here they chose the crossing points to the coastal cities. Thus caravan stations developed in the valley, preferably at places with a year-round water supply. Such favoured locations, one of which was Baalbek, became agricultural centres.

The main route through Baalbek ran in ancient times in a north–south direction just as it does today. In the *Itinerarium Antoninum* we find a road from

Emesa (Homs) through Heliopolis (Baalbek) to Abila (Souk Wadi Barada) and Damascus. To this road belonged a milestone found in 1906 near Yabbule. It was erected by Valerius Constantius and Galerius Maximianus in A.D. 305 and gives a distance of 27 km (17 miles) to Baalbek.

There are two direct routes from Baalbek to the coast, one through Yammune, Afka and Akura to Jbeil (Byblos) and one past the Cedars and Beharre to Tripolis, both of them through difficult mountain terrain. Thus Baalbek is not a crossroads but a link in the routes connecting Tripolis with Damascus and Palmyra with Beirut.

In short, Baalbek was a natural centre for the upper part of the Beqa'a, being located at its highest level, at the source of two important rivers, and on the main inland transportation road parallel to the coast.

The name Baalbek is Semitic and is unmistakably related to the great Semitic God Baal. The most widely accepted definition of the name was offered by Renan, who thought that it simply means Lord of the Beqa'a (Baal meaning 'lord' or master). In any case, what is certain is that the name is of ancient Canaanite origin and that a city existed which was connected with the cult of Baal and which probably served as a religious centre of the Beqa'a.

There is little archaeological evidence to throw light on the origin of the site. Of course we know from the general history of the area about the presence of the Canaanites, Aramaeans, Assyrians, Neo-Babylonians and Persians, but in Baalbek there are few traces of them. Recent excavations in the Great Court of the Temple of Jupiter revealed the existence of a *tell*, containing evidence of human life back to the Early Bronze Age (2900–2300 B.C.). The numerous rock-cut tombs around the town may date back as far as Phoenician times, but they were all robbed of their contents long ago.

The invasion of Asia by Alexander the Great brought about the Hellenization of this part of the world. After his death in 323 B.C. and the division of his empire, Phoenicia was contested by the Ptolemies and Seleucids. After long struggles Phoenicia and Coele-Syria passed into the hands of the Seleucid kings (198 B.C.). The subsequent weakness of the Seleucids caused continuous unrest in the area; from 83 to 69 B.C. Phoenicia was ruled by the Armenian king Tigranes, and after a short succession by Antiochus XII Asiaticus, the last of the Seleucids (69 to 65 B.C.), the Roman general Pompey burst on the scene. Josephus tells us of his march to Damascus through the Beqa'a: 'He destroyed the fortress of Lysias, of which the Jew Silas was Lord. And passing the cities of Heliopolis and Chalcis, he crossed the mountain that divided the region called Coele-Syria from the rest of Syria and came to Damascus.'

Chalcis, today's Majdel Anjar, was the political capital of the Beqa'a, while Heliopolis (Baalbek) was its religious centre. Strabo places Heliopolis and Chalcis close to Apamea. He also tells us of the Ituraeans, who terrorized caravan trade from strongholds in the mountains. They are the first Arabic-speaking people mentioned in the area.

The name Heliopolis given to Baalbek is a clear indication of its importance

The ruins of Baalbek from the south-east

during Seleucid or even Ptolemean times. It is a purely Greek term, meaning City of the Sun (Helios = Sun; Polis = City). It remained the city's name until the end of the Byzantine era. To distinguish it from its important namesake in Lower Egypt writers used to specify 'in Phoenicia' or 'in the Lebanon'.

Pompey incorporated into the new province of Syria both Lebanon and Palestine. Due to the strategic importance of the area it was placed under a proconsul who had the power to levy troops and engage in war. In 47 B.C. Julius Caesar passed through the province and conferred privileges on certain coastal cities. Mark Antony, who in the division of the Roman world received the East, passed on to Queen Cleopatra, last of the Ptolemies, the eastern Mediterranean coastlands, including the Beqa'a. After a short incursion by the Parthians, Antony's generals regained the territory and in 31 B.C. Octavian, triumvir and future emperor, chased Antony and Cleopatra from Syria. When the senate conferred on him the title of Augustus in 27 B.C., the Roman world finally entered its golden age of peace and stability, commonly known as the Pax Romana. Berytus (Beirut) became a Roman colony, which in the beginning included Heliopolis. It is in this context that the construction of the Roman Temples at Baalbek was begun.

CHAPTER THREE

The Religious Heritage

Regional Origins

THE first settlers in the area appeared during early Neolithic times (*c.* 6000 B.C.). One important consequence of community life was the impetus given to the evolution of religious thought. During his pastoral stage the Middle Easterner was a devotee of the moon god, in whose cool light flocks could comfortably graze. In the following agricultural stage the obvious association between growth and sun was established. Parallel to this, the belief in some deities associated with the tribe or the land and the concept of a life after death will have developed.

The more man established permanent agricultural communities, the more he realized the importance of the climatic cycle and the interdependence of sun, soil and rain. To the worship of the sun god, man added the worship of the earth mother, of a goddess of fertility and gods representing spring, rain and tempests. Thus through the ages the Canaanites and Phoenicians, like the Egyptians and Babylonians, developed a definite pantheon, and a religion which greatly influenced the lives of the people.

To the excavation of Ras Shamra (Ugarit) by Claude Schaeffer we owe a fair knowledge of the religion of the Semitic tribes in Western Syria, including Phoenicia. The Library of King Niqmad yielded a treasure of information on predominantly religious subjects. The tablets contain magic formulae associated mainly with fertility cults. Numerous idols with exaggerated female attributes depict fertility goddesses.

The supreme god of the Canaanites was El, the sun god, who also carried the bull as an attribute. He represents the agricultural basis of society. The sea-oriented branch of society is represented by El's wife, Ashera, goddess of the sea. This supreme couple could not be approached directly but only through the mediation of a 'family member', their son Baal (lord). He was the master of rain, tempest and thunder. His symbols were a thunderbolt ending in a spear, ears of corn, and again the bull, shared with his father. Baal had a son, Aliyan, who was the god of springs and floral growth, and a daughter, Anat, who was Aliyan's faithful lover.

Against these positive forces was posed Mot (death), the god of summer and drought, who not only brought all fruit to ripeness but also killed the vegetation, if not supported by Aliyan's springs. In addition there was Astarte, the promiscuous goddess of love and general fertility.

Reflecting the cycle of nature in a region with a marked contrast between a rich period of growth precipitated by the rainy winter and the inevitable death of most vegetation caused by the summer drought – unless elaborate irrigation systems were developed – Canaanite mythology is one of death and resurrection. Baal and Aliyan rule the earth during winter and spring with torrents, storms, lightning and thunder. But when precipitation stops and springs reduce their flow, Mot attains superiority and kills first Baal, then his son. Before Aliyan's defeat, at the peak of nature's richness, the young god enters into an orgy of love. His sister and lover, Anat, retrieves his body from the underworld and buries it. Then she searches for Mot and asks him to bring Aliyan back to life. When he refuses, she kills him in a fight, which suggests the harvest:

> *Anat seized Mot, the divine son,*
> *with a sickle she cut him,*
> *with a winnow she winnows him,*
> *with fire she scorches him,*
> *with a mill she crushes him,*
> *she scatters his flesh in the field to be eaten by birds,*
> *so that his destiny may be fulfilled.*

With the destruction of Mot the summer heat recedes, and in late autumn Baal and Aliyan reappear.

The sequence of life and death expressed in this mythology is duplicated in the cult of Adonis and Osiris. The Adonis cult flourished until Roman times and, as the cycle of life and death also embraced man, it stressed the sexual aspects of life. Thus ritual prostitution was believed to induce increased fertility in animals and plants. In the more cosmopolitan coastal cities such rites may very well have degenerated into debased forms of promiscuity, which to this day tarnish pagan forms of worship in the eyes of the western world.

What we can discern from the above is a basic triad of gods, Baal, Aliyan and Anat, in a father–son–daughter relationship. Baal was adopted by the Assyrians as Bel, and he can be equated with the Egyptian Seth, the Phoenician Reshef and the Aramaean Haddad. Triads of the kind we can again recognize in Zeus, Hermes and Aphrodite or Jupiter, Mercury and Venus.

The Heliopolitan Triad

The nature of the Heliopolitan triad is established by inscriptions, carved representations and numismatic evidence found in various parts of the Roman Empire. They attest to the widespread acceptance of the cult which was most likely disseminated by Syrian merchants and soldiers. Let us not forget also that whole dynasties of Roman emperors were of Syrian origin. Usually reference is made to Iovi Optimo Maximo et Veneri et Mercurio Heliopolitanis. Whether all three gods were worshipped together in the Sanctuary of Jupiter or each had its proper temple cannot be ascertained.

Since Jupiter Heliopolitan was the most important of them we know most about his attributes. First of all there was the famous statue of the god which used to stand in the temple dedicated to him. The only known description of it is given by the fifth century writer Macrobius who calls the god *Zeus Heliopolitanus*. According to him the statue was of gold, representing a beardless person, holding in his right hand a whip, like a charioteer, and in his left a thunderbolt with ears of corn. In the statuettes left to us he is usually depicted wearing a huge *calathos* on his head, symbol of his divinity, and being flanked by two bulls, a Syrian heritage. Generally reference is made to him as *Iovi Optimo Maximo Heliopolitano*, 'Jupiter, the Most High and the Most Great of Heliopolis'.

Probably the best preserved representation of the god comes from Baalbek and is now in the Musée du Louvre. Besides the usual attributes, the figure displays a winged sun disc on the chest – a possible reference to the god of Egyptian Heliopolis. Below, the figure is clad with seven reliefs depicting the seven planets of Roman astrology: Helios the sun god, Selene the moon goddess, Mars and Mercury, Jupiter and Venus and Saturn.

The Religious Rites

Of the actual forms of worship we know little. There are indications that in early times human sacrifice and ritual dedication of women to temples were practised. As a rule, the sources of good things were worshipped with prayers and sacrifices presided over by the priests, whereas the forces of evil were combated with ceremonies of riddance, inviting more active forms of group dances and rites which easily turned into orgiastic festivals. Certainly, the sacrifice of animals and the offering of produce was normal practice, involving ablution in sacred pools, burning on altars with the smoke dissolving in the atmosphere, or slaughtering in places where the blood would enter crevices and merge with the earth.

This twofold religious activity is very significant. The disciplined worship of the good forces, open to everybody willing to participate, at any time, was the official form of religious practice. On the other hand, the group activities of riddance had a more secret character, involving elaborate rites designed to compensate fear, dissolve complexes and lift the initiated to supernatural experiences, possibly involving the use of intoxicating drugs and liquids. This may be the key to the curious duality of temples in Baalbek.

As a rule, the rites of sacrifice and worship were outdoor activities, not requiring elaborate structures, but rather secluded courtyards. High places were also favoured for ceremonies, and the significance of the physical location was certainly grasped from the start.

Bronze statue of
Jupiter Heliopolitan,
height 38.4cm (Musée
du Louvre, Charles
Sursock Collection)

BAALBEK

The majestic mountains of Lebanon, their summits shrouded in clouds and covered with snow for many months of the year, their flanks overgrown with dense forests of stately cedars, their gorges studded with gushing, sparkling torrents, these mountains were not only an obstacle to overcome but also a scenic experience which gave rise to spiritual speculation. A more appropriate setting for the abode of gods who represented such material phenomena as rain and tempest, fertility and growth, would be difficult to imagine. Situated near the highest point of the Beqa'a, controlling the watershed between the Orontes river to the north, and the Leontes river to the south, Baalbek combined aspects of a city in a plain with that of a high-place, and was thus predestined to become a centre of religious worship.

Architecture for Religion

Early forms of worship always developed around some sort of natural feature, such as springs, peculiar rock formations, or – as seems to be the case in Baalbek – a natural crevice. Of actual temple construction we read very little in the records. The Ras Shamra tablets tell of Ashera's request that El should allow the construction of a temple for Baal, and after El had received a throne and stool from Hayin, god of the artisans, he granted permission. In Byblos we find remains of a sanctuary dated about 600 B.C., the so-called Temple of the Obelisks. It is composed of a cella (the temple interior) upon a podium in the centre of a courtyard. The cella contains a stone pedestal for the cult object. All these elements we shall find in the Roman temple scheme for Baalbek.

The most elaborate temple scheme of Semitic tradition was the Temple of Solomon (963 to 923 B.C.) in Jerusalem. Nothing of it remains but a detailed, if sometimes confusing, description. We read in the Bible (I, Kings, 5–7) that the Phoenicians supplied the design, know-how and timber for the construction of the Temple: 'Hiram, king of Tyre, sent his servants to Solomon . . . they hew cedar trees out of Lebanon . . .' An enclosed sacred area with courtyards was created. The temple itself, conceived as a house, was an oblong building which consisted of three sections: the porch (ulam), the holy hall (hekhal), and the holy of holies (debir). This triple division has its counterpart in the Egyptian temples. The Phoenicians, themselves under strong Egyptian influence, had long used this design. Two separate columns of bronze flanked the porch, a feature recalling the two columns seen by Herodotus in Melkart's Temple at Tyre. The hall was used for daily services during which the priests burned incense and made propitiatory offerings of bread. Behind this space, but on a higher level, was the debir, its folding door of wood remaining closed except on the Day of Atonement. All public activities of worship took place outside in the court, which was furnished with bronze altars for animal sacrifice, bronze basins for ablution and a golden table for the offering of incense.

THE RELIGIOUS HERITAGE

Herod's reconstruction of the temple on a colossal scale reveals more clearly the Semitic features of a sacred precinct which was enlarged to about 300 by 800 m (1000 by 2600 ft). This space was divided into zones which served for a step by step classification of worshippers according to their religious worthiness. An outer court was public, then came the separation of gentiles from Jews, then of women from men, finally of laymen from priests – until we reach the holy of holies which was entered once a year only by the high priest, on the Day of Atonement. Construction started in 20 B.C., and as its fame spread the project must certainly have influenced the designers of Baalbek.

The Semitic sanctuaries suggest a powerful priest class and an emphasis on secrecy and mystery. To close off the outside was basic to the Middle Eastern planning tradition. Faced with a predominantly arid and hot climate, people thought of internal courts, walled-in spaces with private, shaded areas. Embellishments like colonnades faced inwards, the external appearance being secondary. The covered spaces usually began with a porch in front of a hall, with rooms that became more and more private behind. This type of arrangement is known as Bithilani style, apparently developed by the Phoenicians. It is an introverted design, stressing individual safety but providing for the dense grouping of dwellings without loss of privacy. The Semitic design of a place of worship was based upon the same concept, and growing out of its physical environment, it was quite different from that of the Graeco-Roman world.

The Western principle of planning and building is that of the detached, individual house which was developed in the verdant, humid northern reaches. The building material was timber, the roofs were pitched. The freestanding house, open to the inviting surroundings, emphasized the outward appearance of the building. It was something to be looked at from the outside rather than to be experienced from within. A simple porch could be added by an extension of the gable space; the main beam would be carried across and supported by two columns, which demonstrated the effect of columns in front of a wall. The development of the Greek temple faithfully reflects this architectural heritage.

In religious attitude the Western mind also differed markedly from the Oriental. The Greeks particularly had a very natural and direct relationship to their gods who were 'super-human', subject to human weaknesses themselves. The temple was the monumental home of God, a receptacle for his artistic image, but it was not shrouded in mystery. The temple doors were especially designed to admit the early morning sun, which enhanced the view of the statue; the cella was not entered for the ceremonies of worship, and the altar of sacrifice was placed in front of the temple. This arrangement allowed large crowds to take part. During the day, the interior of the temple was not out of bounds and the administering priests were not a privileged class but elected public servants. Architecturally, the Greek temple was not conceived as a container of mystery, expressing the awesome rule of remote gods, but as a symbol of public pride and achievement, a deliberately exposed gift to the god of the community's choice, the symbol of an alliance rather than a submission.

Great care was taken in the open placement of the temple. Access to it was inviting rather than forbidding, and no effort was spared for its exterior embellishment. The Greeks carried this concept so far as to make out of their temples richly decorated monuments that had a very sophisticated spatial relationship with their surroundings and a formal perfection never surpassed. On the other hand, function was neglected: usually equally accessible from all sides, the temple lacked clear expression of front and back; the interior space was cluttered with columns and had no artistic significance – a fully extroverted concept.

The Romans had inherited from the Etruscans a similar Western temple scheme, based on timber construction. However, from the beginning, they stressed the frontality of the temple: they placed it on a podium which was accessible only from the front by a flight of stairs and in addition had a deep columnar porch in front of the cella. This approach created a strong axial relationship which satisfied the Roman taste for order.

The Romans, always thinking in terms of cities, of complete communities, also preferred to integrate the temple into city life, relating it to the forum, if possible, rather than placing it outside the city on a dominating hill, and so (in the Greek sense) creating an acropolis. This very well expressed the Roman notion of religion, not as something apart but as one of the variety of public functions.

The placement of the temple in an open area of the city created a court around and particularly in front of it. This space contained the altar at the foot of the temple steps. However, it was freely accessible and, apart from times of religious festivities, served for everyday activities such as trading. In this way the temple's environs lost their exclusively sacred nature and the temple itself became the permanent place of worship. This factor, in conjunction with the Roman appreciation of internal space in general, made the architects endeavour to improve and embellish the temple's interior. The invention of roof trusses eliminated the need for interior columns and opened the way for a large unobstructed space. Indeed, the most famous of Roman temples, the Pantheon in Rome, is essentially an exquisite interior space only, but its concept as a cylinder topped by a dome with a window in its very centre departed radically from tradition. It was a remarkable exception to the rule because the Romans nowhere adhered more to tradition than in religious architecture. Although they were masters in arch and vault construction, they rarely abandoned the post-and-lintel formula in temple design which they inherited from the Etruscans and Greeks. They also faithfully copied the Greek orders and contented themselves with decorative enrichment and the combination of exotic materials.

In surveying the various religious traditions which influenced the creation of the sanctuaries in Baalbek, we must not overlook the Mesopotamian forms of worship. For long periods of time the Babylonians and Assyrians ruled over the Beqa'a and undoubtedly brought their religious ideas with them. The archi-

General view of the Temple of Jupiter

tectural crystallization of their worship was the ziggurat. It was a high staged tower with ramps or stairways leading to the sanctuary on top. The famous Tower of Babylon was such a ziggurat. It was a representation of the celestial hill crowned by a temple in which a god was supposed to dwell when he came down to earth for the service of humanity. We recognize in it the expression of people who originally came down to the fertile plains from mountainous regions and who were longing for the lost peaks which were to them links between earth and heaven. (The ziggurat did not contain a tomb and therefore differed totally from the Egyptian pyramid.)

A similar tradition of worship from 'High Places' developed among the Nabateans in southern Jordan. This people was in direct contact with the Egyptians from whom they adopted various architectural forms, such as the Egyptian gorge moulding. Lebanon, and the Beqa'a in particular, being on the way to Egypt via the Nabatean territory, adopted sanctuaries which show altars with Egyptian motifs situated on high places, similar to the Nabatean monuments of Petra.

These diverse influences of architectural and religious concepts will help us to understand many peculiar features of the sanctuaries in Baalbek.

CHAPTER FOUR

The Sanctuary of Jupiter Heliopolitan

UNTIL the Arabs linked the Sanctuary of Jupiter Heliopolitan with the adjoining Temple of Bacchus to form a large fortress, it was a self-contained precinct raised above the level of the plain and accessible only by way of the propylaea. Although situated on the north-western outskirts of the town, away from the mountain slopes to the east and not really overlooking the town, the Sanctuary of Jupiter Heliopolitan is often referred to as the Acropolis of Baalbek. The Arabs however call it the Kala'a, which means fortress.

The compound of the Temple of Jupiter covers an area of about 27 000 square metres (6.5 acres), of which 10 000 square metres (2.5 acres) were open courtyards and stairways. The remaining 17 000 square metres (4 acres) were covered with peristyles, exedras and interior spaces. In order to chart the development of so large a complex, let us first consider the original nature of the site.

Pre-Roman Era

Professor Kalayan, the engineer in charge of restorations by the Lebanese Department of Antiquities, writes in his *Notes on the Heritage of Baalbek and the Beqa'a*:

> In the rectangular courtyard, to the south of the temple of Jupiter, there is a natural crevice about fifty metres deep. At the bottom of this crevice there is a small rock cut altar. In all probability this crevice was the centre of the first worship. Pre-Roman construction is confined to the middle part of the rectangular courtyard and contains remnants of the late second millennium B.C. The site was a tell (an artificial hill, usually the site of a city) which grew gradually like other tells of the Beqa'a.

Since the place of veneration – the bottom of the crevice – was hardly accessible and was, in any case, reserved for the high priests only, the need was felt for a larger altar to be situated outside the crevice on the hill. Around it the worshippers were to gather and to offer sacrifice. As time went on, a court was established with a wall enclosing the whole precinct from the outside. At the east end of the court a gateway with a flight of steps between two towers was built to provide an impressive entrance.

The six remaining columns of the Temple of Jupiter resting upon the pre-Roman podium wall. The huge stones in front of it belong to the base course of the intended Roman podium extension. In the foreground are parts of the Temple of Bacchus.

27

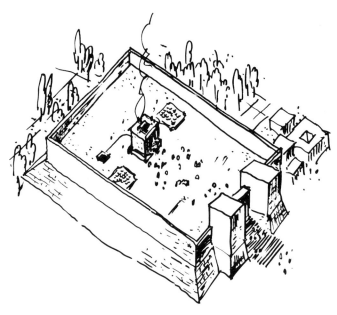

Late in the second millennium B.C., on the site of an ancient settlement, a raised court was built containing the altar of sacrifice. A vertical shaft connects with a natural crevice which opens at the level of the plain. The gateway consists of two towers flanking the stairway.

At the time of the Hellenistic conquest, Baalbek seems to have enjoyed enough fame to attract the attention of the rulers of the day. After the death of Alexander the Great in 323 B.C. the area became part of Ptolemy's Egyptian empire, the centre of which was Alexandria. It seems that the Ptolemies identified the Baal of Baalbek with their sun god and changed the name of the city into Heliopolis. This provided them with a unifying religious centre at the eastern end of the empire. The triad of Baal–Aliyan–Anat was equated with Zeus–Hermes–Aphrodite. Around 200 B.C. the Seleucids under Antiochus the Great won the area from the Ptolemies.

They probably planned to add to the existing courtyard and its altar of sacrifice a temple which, according to their architectural tradition, was designed as an elevated, embellished monument in its own right, towering behind the altar, easily seen by all. Since the sanctuary was already on top of the existing hill, an artificial podium had to be created. Most of this podium had been built when Pompey, the Roman general, occupied Phoenicia and Baalbek in 64 B.C.

Roman Era

The traditional contestants for sovereignty over the Phoenician coast were the great eastern land powers, such as the Babylonians, the Assyrians and the Persians, to whom the Mediterranean coast was a natural limit. In contrast to them the Greeks and Romans came from the west, and their problem was to safeguard this precious coastline against a vast hinterland which they could not hope to control by military means alone. They therefore set out to create a

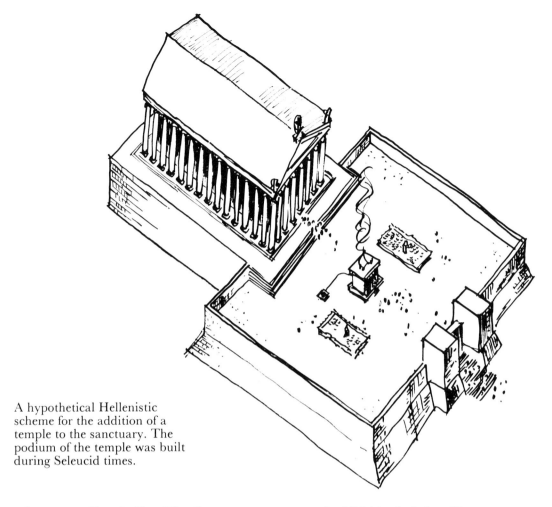

A hypothetical Hellenistic
scheme for the addition of a
temple to the sanctuary. The
podium of the temple was built
during Seleucid times.

safety zone of loyal allies. The Romans were extremely skilful in their handling
of newly acquired lands. They never imposed their will where this was not
absolutely necessary to protect their interests, and avoided everything which
would needlessly alienate newly subjected peoples. They were very tolerant in
matters of faith and religion; they applied their detached political thinking to
this question and acknowledged that gods were the expression of the people
who worshipped them. Thus they recognized the possibility of consolidating
their rule by careful identification with gods of local worship, hoping to unify
the local peoples through unification of their elements of worship.

In the case of Baalbek the first step in this direction was the association of the
local deities with equivalents of their own, such as Jupiter with Baal-Haddad as
supreme god, Venus with Anat or Atargatis and Mercury with Aliyan. Yet, the
Romans had underestimated the appeal of the Middle-Eastern religions which
touched every chord of sensibility and satisfied a thirst for religious emotion that

the austere Roman creed had been unable to quench. Again I quote Professor Kalayan:

> When the Roman Empire conquered the Middle East, the religious aspirations of the Middle East subdued the population of the Mediterranean Roman world. The first goddess to invade Rome was Atargatis. The temples at Niha in the Beqa'a are dedicated to Atargatis. Later we find Adonis and the triad of Baalbek established in Rome. It was through these and other gods of the Orient that the idea of an after-life, with the promise of eternal happiness for the pious and punishment for the wicked, was developed and introduced into the religion of the Mediterranean world. The oriental religions paved the way for the concept of a suffering, loving, universal God. The oriental gods were "all powerful", "everlasting", "most high", "preservers of the whole universe". They were "separated from man by a far greater interval than any god of Greece or Rome".

We witness a reflection of this development in architecture and, not surprisingly, the scheme of the Acropolis in Baalbek represents a mixed product, with Oriental concepts of planning underlying the construction of buildings in the forms of Graeco-Roman tradition. But what was characteristically Roman, because only they could afford it at that time, was the immense scale of the design. In this respect they may have been inspired by the site they found, as well as by their own ambition to outshine all previous sanctuaries.

To take one example, the fact that large portions of the wallfaces of the existing temple podium are carefully finished in smooth rustication is proof that the present foundation wall of Jupiter's temple was once meant to be the finished podium of the Seleucids. If this podium had been designed to receive a temple in the Greek manner, with stairs all round it, its width would have been only 35 or 40 m (115 or 132 ft). The Romans, however, used the podium to build the greatest possible temple on it, placing the columns of the exterior peristyle flush with the face of the wall, thus obtaining a width of 48 m (157 ft) and a length of nearly 90 m (295 ft). Given that basic decision, all else was a question of proportion. There is strong evidence that all parts of the scheme, the spacing of columns, the height of the temple, the distance of the surrounding buildings, the size of the courtyard in front, were subject to strict geometric rules. Accordingly, the Great Court had to be brought into proportion with the design of the temple by drastically extending the tell to the north and south.

Already at this time – the time of Augustus – the fame of Baalbek seems to have been based on an oracle which had its abode in the courtyard. According to Macrobius, of the early fifth century A.D., the oracle expressed itself through the movements of the statue of the god, which was carried on a litter by dignitaries of the province, who had their heads shaven and had previously practised long abstinence.

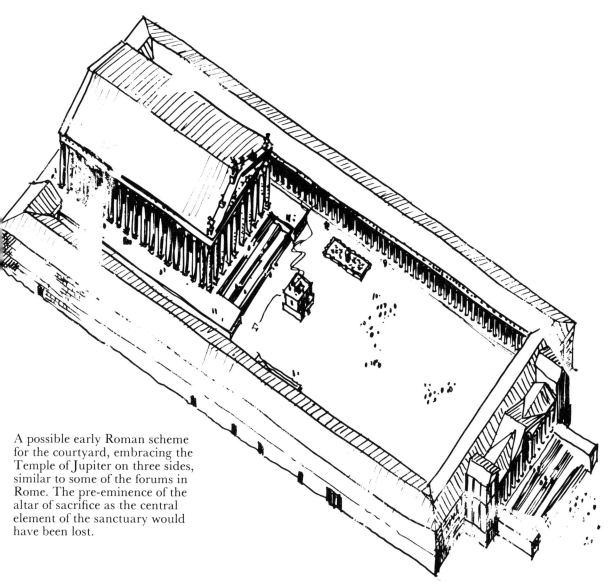

A possible early Roman scheme
for the courtyard, embracing the
Temple of Jupiter on three sides,
similar to some of the forums in
Rome. The pre-eminence of the
altar of sacrifice as the central
element of the sanctuary would
have been lost.

According to Professor Kalayan, the Temple of Jupiter and its courtyard
were planned as a whole. During the Augustan era it became customary in
Rome also to place the temple inside a court, although usually at the far end of
it. In Baalbek this would have resulted in an area about 300 by 130 m (1000 by
400 ft), comparable to the great court schemes of Jerusalem, Damascus or
Palmyra. Professor Kalayan maintains that the Romans planned to build a
courtyard centrally placed in relation to the altar of sacrifice. However, in the
first half of the first century A.D. the courtyard was stopped in line with the
temple facade, although foundations had already been placed for a further

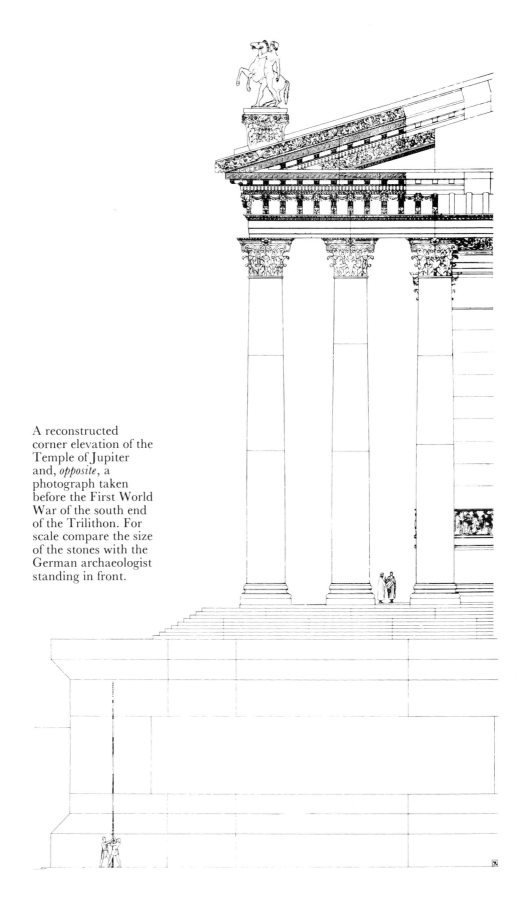

A reconstructed corner elevation of the Temple of Jupiter and, *opposite*, a photograph taken before the First World War of the south end of the Trilithon. For scale compare the size of the stones with the German archaeologist standing in front.

stretch along the north side of the temple. This suspension of construction was probably the result of the excessive effort required to achieve a rather questionable architectural result. In fact, a continuation of the court would have made the temple much less impressive, particularly when viewed from the side of the plain. Instead, the temple was furnished with a monumental extension of the podium which, according to Phoenician tradition, had to consist of no more than three layers of stone. It is not certain whether the Romans had developed such a taste for magnitude that they obligingly accepted this tradition, or whether the local builders insisted on it. The fact remains that this decision involved the cutting, transporting and lifting of the largest and heaviest stones of all times. Not only had a wall 12 m (39 ft) high to be composed of three ranges of stones, but in the interest of appearance the middle blocks were made of a length four times their height. And with a depth equal to the height, the volume amounted to 400 m³ (14000 ft³) per block, corresponding to a weight of almost 1000 tons. Technically the builders of Baalbek proved themselves capable, since three such blocks of the middle layer are in place, but in another sense they did not succeed – the podium remained incomplete. Nevertheless, so awe-inspiring were those blocks to all beholders ever after that Baalbek was known for a long time primarily as the site of the three stones, 'the trilithon', and for centuries people believed that these blocks had been placed there by superhuman giants.

When recently the top of the Trilithon was cleared of rubble it was discovered that this surface had been used as a drawing board for the design of the pediment above. The exact elevation of the raking cornice and the entablature is carved into the stone, and it is clear that the blocks for the construction of the pediment were prepared by means of this full-scale plan. Accordingly,

the Trilithon must have been in place before the entablature of the temple, and particularly its pediment, had been built. On the other hand a discarded column drum, once intended for the Temple of Jupiter, has been used in the foundation *below* the Trilithon, which proves that temple and podium were executed at the same time. All this must have happened in the first half of the first century because the temple was nearing completion in the year A.D. 60 during the reign of Nero, as indicated by an inscription on top of a column shaft. This is one of the rare instances we have of a definite reference date on the construction of the Temple.

Let us return to the Great Court. It seems to have been upon Trajan's visit to the shrine around A.D. 115, when he consulted the oracle before his Parthian campaign, that final decisions about the design of the court were reached. Trajan was carrying out a spectacular building programme in Rome and had appointed Appollodoros of Damascus as chief architect. This must have increased the Oriental influence on architecture. The Forum of Trajan reflects this in its succession of courts, and above all in the introduction of the basilica as a static, transverse space – a typically Eastern element. Trajan may very well have had Appollodoros with him in Baalbek.

Of the oracle the emperor demanded to know whether he would return safely from his campaign against the Parthians. As a reply he received a broken centurion's staff wrapped in a shroud; and indeed, after an inconclusive war Trajan fell ill, died in Cilicia in A.D. 117, and his bones were brought back to Rome.

Hadrian visited Baalbek around A.D. 130 and, being a gifted architect himself to whom building was a real passion, he certainly would have reviewed the plans and given his encouragement. At this time the temple was already in use, although the decorations were still being carved. The interior was probably completed first. All this we can only conjecture from comparison with the wholly preserved Temple of Bacchus. The famous statue of Jupiter Heliopolitan would have been placed at the rear end of the temple in a raised adytum (holy of holies).

With the addition of the Temple of Jupiter, the original altar of sacrifice, which was once the nucleus of the sanctuary, became the usual accessory to a Roman temple. To maintain the local tradition of a High Place as centre of sacrifice, a new and dominating monument was introduced, placed centrally in relation to the whole design. It took the form of a cube-shaped tower 17 m (56 ft) high. The interior of the tower was specifically designed to facilitate the ascent and descent of many people by the skilful arrangement of stairs in two completely independent flights, obviously one set for climbing up, the other for going down. The ceilings of the stairways and corridors were richly carved to impress the visitors, and the deeply worn condition of the treads testifies to the heavy use of the stairs.

We do not know exactly when the tower was built, but judging from the style of the ceiling decorations it must have been soon after the Temple of Jupiter.

34

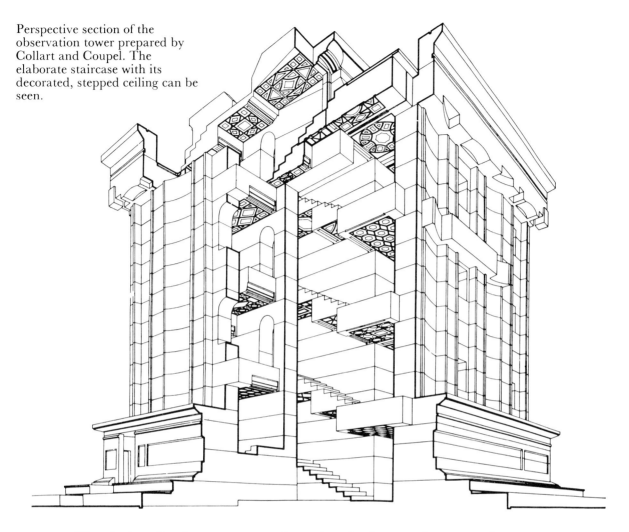

Perspective section of the observation tower prepared by Collart and Coupel. The elaborate staircase with its decorated, stepped ceiling can be seen.

The placing of such a structure on the main axis of approach to a temple was unheard of in Roman architecture, and it is another indication of the eastern disposition of the whole sanctuary. Not only did the construction of the tower restore the previous arrangement of a main altar of sacrifice independent of the temple, but its top also offered a superb view of the god's statue in the rear part of the temple. Indeed, the observation of the glittering image through the wide, open door, when the rays of the rising sun were penetrating the darkness of the cella, must have been the climax of a pilgrimage.

The Phoenician influence on planning seems to have been matched by a very large participation in the financing of the work, so large indeed that no emperor claims credit for having constructed or even contributed to the construction of the Temple of Jupiter. The area was in fact one of the richest of the whole empire – the Beqa'a being frequently called 'the Granary of Rome'. We

A view of the Great Court
towards the Temple of Jupiter.
To the left are remains of the
observation tower with
pre-Roman work in front. To the
right, a solitary column, a basin
for ablution and the enclosing
exedra. The pointed arches in the
background are Arab fortification
works.

A Roman coin depicting the
Propylaeum of the Temple of
Jupiter

A reconstructed elevation of the
Propylaea. Flanking towers
remind us of Egyptian temple
pylons or Babylonian city gates.
The combination of architrave,
arch and pediment is typically
Syrian.

can deduce that the local people fully regarded the Heliopolitan Jupiter as their own superior god, who carried all the attributes of Baal-Haddad.

Still, the progress of work on the Great Court seems not to have been rapid. Under the wise rule of Hadrian (A.D. 117–138), the Roman Empire had become well consolidated, and with his carefully chosen successor, Antoninus Pius (A.D. 138–161), the empire entered into a period of peace and wealth. The provinces particularly enjoyed a marked prosperity; trade flourished, and it must have been a golden era for Syria.

At the same time eastern influences were increasingly apparent in the empire, particularly in the spiritual realm. For instance, the cult of Dionysos or Bacchus became so important that Antoninus Pius decided to start a completely new temple, also of huge dimensions, next to the Acropolis. The second half of the second century was therefore occupied with the continuation of the court on the Acropolis and the construction of the so-called Temple of Bacchus.

After a short period of unrest, Septimius Severus (A.D. 193–211) reorganized the province of Syria and, according to Ulpian, divided Syria in A.D. 195 and bestowed upon Baalbek the *jus italicum*. With this decree Baalbek moved into the prominent class of Roman communities. Construction activity was at a peak, and many coins struck during his rule depict the sanctuary of Jupiter Heliopolitan.

As work on the Great Court progressed plans were drawn up for the great Propylaea which would furnish the Acropolis with an adequate entrance. It is interesting to note that their design is a magnified version of the propylaeum to the pre-Roman sanctuary. Originally, the propylaeum was to be on ground level, giving access to a small rectangular forecourt from where a stairway would have led to the elevated Great Court. After construction along these

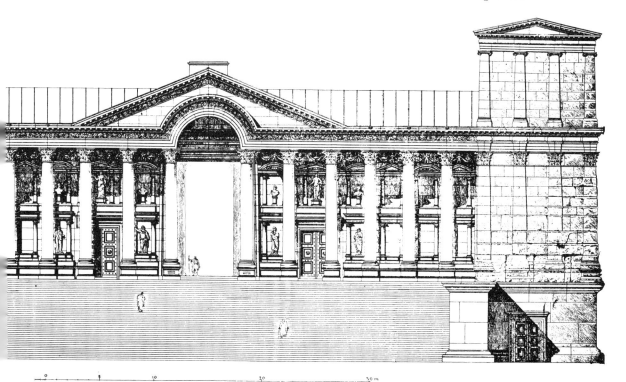

The Hexagonal Court, looking towards the
Propylaeum. The inner line of stones marks the
position of the peristyle to which the roof once
extended. The vaults and upper parts of the walls
are Arab fortification works.

lines was begun, it was decided to raise the forecourt to the same level as the
Great Court and to enlarge it thereby. The propylaea were equally raised and
now received a monumental stairway in front of them. During the rule of
Caracalla (A.D. 211–217) – foremost member of the Syrian dynasty of emperors
– construction continued, with the stress on the Propylaea, as indicated by

inscriptions on the pedestals of portico columns, which reveal to us that an officer of the First Legion Antonianus had the bronze capitals of these columns gilded at his expense for the safety of the Emperor Caracalla and his mother Julia Domna.

This inscription does not mean that the court behind the Propylaea was finished: indeed the whole complex was never fully completed. Several years later Philip the Arab (A.D. 244–249), who had the finished Propylaea depicted on coins, was able to make a last minute change in the scheme. Philip came from the Hauran and must have been thoroughly steeped in local religious tradition. To him the aspect of an immense sacred area accessible directly from the outside world, with such ease of approach to the sanctuary, would have been disconcerting. Was it not much more appropriate to enter gradually into a sanctuary of such importance, to introduce a self-centred buffer zone, an area of reflection and contemplation after passing through the monumental gateway? No more fitting solution could have been found than the creation of the Hexagonal Forecourt, a feature unique in Roman design and of a decidedly Oriental flavour. Next to the circle or octagon, the hexagon is the most balanced and centred space configuration. It discourages a casual stroll and automatically makes a visitor pause.

Most recent findings revealed a ceremonial plaza in front of the Propylaea. It is delimited by a low wall with a sort of continuous stone bench on the inside which connects to the outer corners of the propylaeum towers and terminates in a large semicircle. Foundations for various monuments on this plaza are in evidence, as is an elaborate drainage system. This way the scheme was extended by another seventy metres, attaining an overall length of 340 metres (1100 feet).

Many details in the ground level chambers, between the two courtyards, attest to alteration, demolitions and omissions, which were occasioned by the changes in planning. Unfortunately, there are no inscribed dates or other evidence which provide exact information on the chronological sequence of the construction.

The tentative dating of the various parts is derived from stylistic comparison in the decorative details. But this can be misleading, since decorations were added after the buildings had been erected.

The middle of the third century again witnessed much activity. Coins of Valerianus (A.D. 253–260) and Gallienus (A.D. 253–268) mention the continuation of the festivals of Baalbek: 'TESTAMEN SACRUM CAPETOLINUM OECOMENICUM ISSELASTICUM HELIOPOLITANUM' (The Holy Capitoline Games of the Universal Heliopolitan Festival). However, this does not necessarily mean that the construction work had been completed. It was customary to inaugurate such monumental sanctuaries as soon as rough masonry was up, while all the time-consuming surface decoration was applied in subsequent years. Consequently, when Emperor Constantine in A.D. 330 declared Christianity the official religion of the Roman state, building activity came to an abrupt halt and many details were left unfinished.

CHAPTER FIVE

The Temple of Bacchus

The Dedication and Purpose of the Temple

Among the extensive remains at Baalbek, the Temple of Bacchus is particularly well preserved. It is, in fact, the best preserved Roman temple of this size anywhere. Yet, curiously, very little is known about the dedication and purpose of this magnificent building. Strictly speaking, we should refer to it as the 'so-called' Temple of Bacchus, because the dedication of the building to this joyous god is far from certain. However, there is a prior question: why was this temple built at all?

The temple stands in a curious relationship – or better non-relationship – to the great complex of the Temple of Jupiter, commonly called the Acropolis of Baalbek because of its elevated position. This acropolis, with its overpowering size and lofty location, is a complete entity and certainly must have been connected in some significant way with the town of Baalbek. The towering Temple of Jupiter is at the end of an enormous axis of movement which sweeps

40

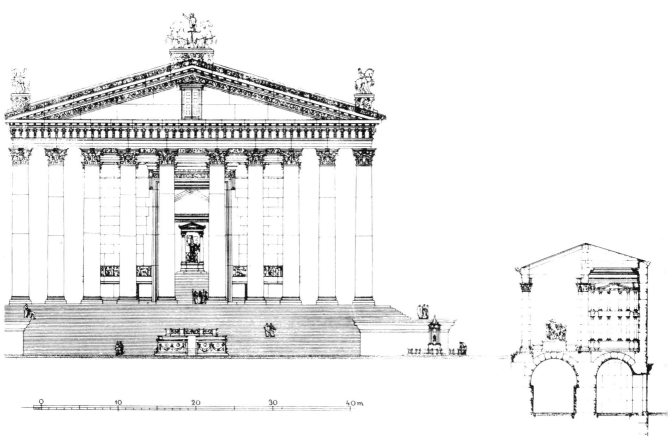

Transverse section through the Acropolis, looking west

all the way past the immense courtyards to the Propylaea and reaches down their steps to attract the eager pilgrims to the shrine of the supreme god whom the Romans conceived as a fusion of Jupiter and the local god Haddad. The scale of the ensemble is so colossal that the whole city is dwarfed by it. No structure could have competed with it. The natural thing to do was to relate to it lesser sanctuaries in a fashion that paid tribute to the master of the heavens. A good example of such a solution is the Temple of Venus, which is turned towards the acropolis, although it originally shared the space of a rather crowded court with another small temple.

And yet, here is the Temple of Bacchus, a huge building by any standards, resting strangely in the shadow of the acropolis, pushed nearly to the end of the forbidding wall which supports the Great Court. Its position is such that we cannot believe its columns are but 2·5 m (8 ft) shorter than those remaining six giants of Jupiter's Temple, dramatically exposed against the brilliant sky.

BAALBEK

Why should anybody have engaged in such a costly undertaking against such competition? Obviously there must have been compelling reasons, and they must have been intended to satisfy a religious need.

When the Temple of Bacchus was begun, now commonly assumed to have been at the time of Antoninus Pius in the middle of the second century A.D., the Temple of Jupiter had already been completed, except for the projected extension of its podium. By that time the sanctuary of Jupiter Heliopolitan had gained great repute in the Roman world, largely because of the oracle connected with it. The creation of the acropolis of Baalbek had above all been a political act initiated by the imperial government with the aim of outshining or absorbing the strong religious traditions of the area and thereby effectively consolidating the rule of Rome. It was to be a demonstration of the power of Roman state religion and was designed to establish the predominance of that religion once and for all.

However, if the Romans supposed that they could overwhelm the oriental spirit with sheer material magnitude they were mistaken. The spiritually much more developed eastern cults exercised an emotional power which the rather sober Roman beliefs could not match. The eastern belief promising rewards in an after-life greatly appealed to the Roman legionary, who, far from home, was exposed to the uncertainties of a military career. He brought the new ideas back to Rome, and soon they successfully infiltrated the western provinces and imperial Rome itself.

One of the favourite local cults was the veneration of the Greek god Dionysos, the youthful and handsome god of wine and drama, identified with the Roman god Bacchus. Worship centred around the elements of sowing and creating, harvesting and feasting. What was originally an agricultural appreciation of the life cycle had gradually developed into more sophisticated notions of continuous death and re-creation, and under the growing influence of Christianity the concept of resurrection may have evolved.

Henri Seyrig writes:

> The two or three centuries under the rule of Greek kings were a time of extraordinary religious fertility, antedating the rise of Christianity. Above all the questions related to life after death were important to the minds of the believers, and the ancient fertility cults which once were to bring about the return of spring changed into mystic cults in which the idea of resurrection was cultivated and where from the example of certain gods man drew the hope of a rebirth after death. Among the mysteries offering such promise those of Dionysos or Bacchus were particularly successful, and the Phoenician cities believed they recognized in him their youthful god Adonis. In Baalbek this god of rejuvenation was first equated with Hermes by the Greeks, then the development of the mysteries brought about his personification as Bacchus.

THE TEMPLE OF BACCHUS

The very character of this cult seems to have stressed certain philosophies and rituals requiring individual participation by each member – a radical departure from anonymous mass worship and ritual sacrifice before the official god of the state. It may be that membership was limited and granted only after a period of initiation. If this is true, then such a cult would not be compatible with a sanctuary open to anybody but must have been accommodated in an independent structure. And indeed, does not the Temple of Bacchus appear to defy its greater brother on the acropolis, claiming independence by having its own separate approach, which once featured several flights of steps now buried?

It may be that attraction to the cult of Bacchus was so strong at the time of Antoninus Pius that the emperor felt it wise to start a separate sanctuary. But there are also indications that the building was financed by the cities of the area, supporting the theory that the project was of particular local concern. For instance, it is established that one ceiling panel depicts the patron god of Antioch, an honour most certainly awarded to the city in return for financial support.

The first person to suggest the attribution of the temple to Bacchus was the German archaeologist Otto Puchstein. His theory was based on the carvings around the door of the temple and particularly those belonging to the adytum or inner shrine. To the right and left of the flight of stairs leading to the adytum are two blocks of stone which once supported the adytum structure. The faces of these blocks carried two reliefs which unfortunately are now badly defaced. In spite of their condition Otto Puchstein presented a convincing interpretation, which is shown in the illustration.

Reliefs at the entrance to the adytum.
Above, the right half shows the birth of Dionysos. Zeus sinks down bending backward, his knee nearly touching the ground. Hermes to the left comes to his aid, leaning forward and receiving the child which is coming forth through Zeus' side. On the left, between two pairs of satyrs and bacchantes dancing to the music of a flute player, little Dionysos is sitting on a small panther. *Below*, in the middle, a dancing satyr and two maenads followed by two servants carrying a large jug of wine. To the right, a group of people with Dionysos, leaning on a vine, holding a rhyton in his right hand.

BAALBEK

However, there is also evidence which seems to contradict the attribution of the temple to Bacchus. For example, on the underside of the lintel over the gate we see an eagle holding a caduceus in his claws – the symbol of Mercury. Also, if we want to consider the triad of gods referred to in inscriptions, Mercury would have been second to Jupiter in importance and should have received a temple more centrally located than the one on Sheikh Abdallah hill.

There remains the theory that the temple was not dedicated to one particular god at all, but to a cult. The abundance of purely symbolic decoration would support this view. There is one point I would like to stress: that the polytheistic era preceding Christianity was one of great and sustained piety. The eastern cults distinguished themselves by their universalist nature which made them radiate beyond the local limits. From reliefs and sculpture found as far away as Marseilles and Nîmes we know that the cult of Jupiter Heliopolitan was on an international scale. It must have contained some important message, possibly growing out of the close contact with Judaism and Christianity, a message which harmonized with this important time of transition from polytheistic concepts. Franz Cumont has the following to say on this subject:

> Solar pantheism, which grew up among the Syrians of the Hellenistic period as a result of the influence of Chaldean astrolatry, imposed itself upon the whole Roman world under the empire. In this matter Syria was Rome's teacher and predecessor. The last formula reached by the religion of the pagan Semites and in consequence by that of the Romans, was a divinity unique, almighty, eternal, universal and ineffable, that revealed itself throughout nature, but whose most splendid and most energetic manifestation was the sun. To arrive at the Christian monotheism only one final tie had to be broken, that is to say, this supreme being residing in a distant heaven had to be removed beyond the world. So we see once more in this instance, how the propagation of the Oriental cults levelled the roads for Christianity and heralded its triumph.

In the absence of written records we cannot know details of those cults, and there is little hope that complete answers will be found to these questions. Too much evidence was destroyed subsequently; so much, in fact, that none of the excavations have brought forth a single statue, although there must have been hundreds of them at one time. Only the sculpture of a seated goddess was found well before excavations started and taken to the Ottoman Museum at Constantinople.

The underside of the lintel over the gate of the adytum. An eagle with a caduceus in his claws is holding garlands in his beak. The ends of the garlands are held by winged genii.

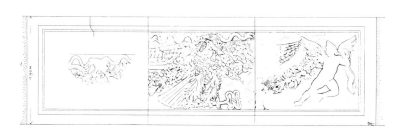

The south-west corner of the
Temple of Bacchus. Precariously
projecting pediment blocks are
held in place by steel and
concrete.

The Architectural Significance of the Temple

In discussing the architectural significance of the Temple of Bacchus, we must
be careful to consider it in its own right, as a piece of architecture deliberately
separated from the acropolis. It was conceived as such and should be so judged.

The most remarkable aspect of the temple now is its admirable state of preservation. Because of this fortunate circumstance it has been possible to make
accurate and complete reconstructions, both in reality and on paper. The temple
is a veritable treasure of scientific investigation. It was found to adhere fully to
the modular proportions specified by Vitruvius, the famous Roman author of
an architectural treatise.

THE TEMPLE OF BACCHUS

Many people consider the temple's large size as its next most significant feature. It is larger than the Parthenon, with a clear interior span of 19 m (62 ft) and a monumental gateway 6.5 m (21 ft) wide and nearly 13 m (42 ft) high. Its blocks of stone generally weigh tens of tons, although still dwarfed by the nearby Temple of Jupiter. Certainly, the grandeur of the conception, the overpowering effect of strength and magnitude, softened somewhat by delightful decoration and proportion, make this temple one of the outstanding examples of sheer size turned into substantive quality.

Nevertheless, I contend that architectural significance has essentially little to do with size and quantity. Is then this temple nothing more than a magnified version of Greek trabeated architecture, an unabashed attempt to outdo the past by magnitude?

Technically, this may be a valid assessment because the post and lintel construction, as expressed in the classical orders and as chosen by the Romans for this temple, was a purely traditional form, essentially limited to more modest dimensions which could be conveniently dealt with in stone. To use this principle of construction on such a scale was a 'tour de force'. Beyond that it was an outdated method for the Roman engineer of the day, whose acquired learning was to cast walls economically in concrete and to span lofty spaces with lasting vaults. The temples of Baalbek reflect much more strongly the vigorous local tradition of monumental masonry construction, which in its technical excellence and physical magnitude has no equal. Solid stone blocks are fitted so precisely that a razor blade cannot enter a joint; whole flights of steps are cut out of single blocks; and repairs of broken parts are done so meticulously as to be practically invisible. All this was done with an intrinsic delight in magnitude and quality.

But let us return to architecture. The features that strike our eyes first are forms, colours and textures. The Temple of Bacchus has an exterior colonnade much like that of the Parthenon. We all know that the Parthenon was the final word in this kind of design, and we will not find in Baalbek such subtleties as slightly tilted columns or curved horizontals, although we must mention here the unequal spacing of columns at the short sides and the ten per cent narrowing of the doorframe towards the top in order to strengthen the visual effect. We also know that the Parthenon was carved out of gleaming white Pentelian marble throughout, a material for which the limestone of Baalbek is no match.

Let us not forget that what we see today on the Acropolis of Athens are the beautifully weathered remains of a perfectionist colonnade once wrapped around a block of cella. Today's transparency gives it a romantic gracefulness which was quite absent at its completion. To this we have to add the bright polychrome treatment of the upper part which is very foreign to our present concept of classical architecture. This we have to contrast with Baalbek's Temple of Bacchus, with its glowing, warm walls and generously bulging columns, its flamboyant Corinthian capitals and boldly projecting cornice, its superb contrast of plain and fluted column shafts and the infinite variety of carving, delicate when seen at close range and vigorous when looming high above us, a rich symphony of

The porch of the Temple of Bacchus showing the gate and the interior

colour, texture and form. Here is an architecture to be experienced by the senses rather than the intellect.

We have looked at the temple and made our comparisons. The next step is to enter, and a decisive step it is. For is not architecture above all the art of defining space, even more of creating space for man to live in? It is the space inside or between our buildings which really matters, the space in which we move through time. It is here that the true significance of the Temple of Bacchus becomes apparent. There is no hesitancy as we ascend the magnificent sweep of stairs reaching out in front of the temple. We enter under the columns of the lofty pronaos and approach with growing expectation the inviting splendour of the gateway, beyond which a magnificent interior space will envelop us, a space uncluttered and open. Columns have been rendered unnecessary by the huge roof trusses of cedarwood. A space articulated by lavish architectural and figural decoration, engaged (that is to say, attached to the wall)

Above, the interior of the Temple of Bacchus with the steps to the adytum. To the left, a richly carved door frame.

Opposite, a reconstruction of the adytum. It demonstrates the effect created by a multiplicity of classical forms arranged in complicated juxtaposition.

THE TEMPLE OF BACCHUS

Corinthian columns on pedestals, carrying an elaborately broken entablature, separating tiers of niches arched or with triangular pediments, a succession of projections and recesses giving vibrant life to the voluminous space defined by it.

Plan, form and space in harmony – this is the key to Roman architecture. Following the concept of an organic whole, the Romans endeavoured to reach plastic and spatial unity within an interrelated composition by subjecting it to the discipline of a great axis and strict symmetry. Furthermore, the interior of the sanctuary proper represents a fully developed space, designed to harmonize with the exteriors and therefore repeating the familiar elements of applied orders with tiers of niches, only on an even richer level.

Traditionally, the ceremonies and sacrifices took place in front of the temple at the altar, particularly at sunrise, when the sun would reach the temple interior and illuminate the cult statue – hence the temple's orientation to the east. With the development of the restricted religious cults, such as that of Bacchus, increasing emphasis might have been placed on the solemn initiation of the believers inside the temple in front of the god. The sudden lack of brilliant sunshine, the diminishing flow of light from the entrance, and the flickering glow of countless oil lamps and candles must have sustained the

powerful mystery expected in the shrine. The raised adytum, or holy of holies, a typical oriental feature, was not accessible to anyone but the priests: it was a temple within the temple, revealing the statue of the god behind veils of incense smoke.

This carefully orchestrated harmony of materials, colours, forms and spaces has a Baroque touch, an artistic attitude far different from that of the classical Greeks and not achieved again until the great masters of the High- and Late-Renaissance.

The Temple of Bacchus represents the remarkable moment of classical architecture where exterior and interior are of equal importance, a condition achieved neither by the exquisite exteriors of Pericles nor the great interiors of antiquity, such as the Pantheon or Haghia Sophia. In Sir Mortimer Wheeler's words:

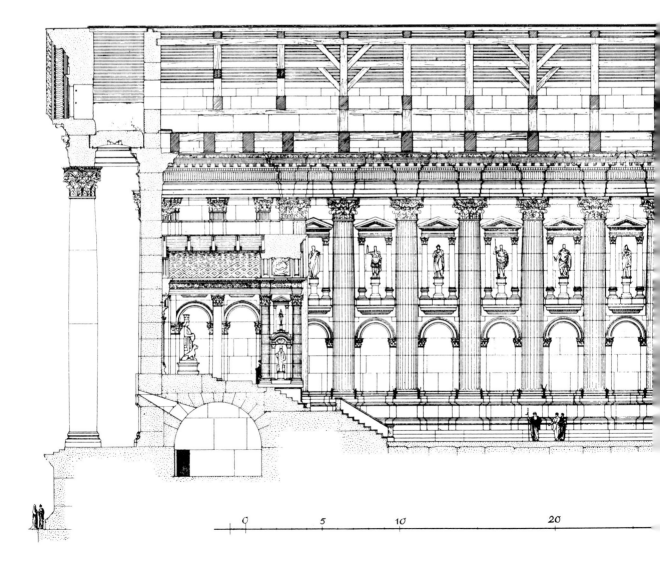

THE TEMPLE OF BACCHUS

Baalbek is the end of one tradition and the beginning of another. Meanwhile it fitted the temper of the world into which it was born. It represents that momentary pause, which might properly be called the 'Antonine pause', in an age of vital transmutation; that moment of balance that was "the period in history of the world during which the condition of the human race was most happy and prosperous". In so doing, and in its own right, Baalbek remains one of the very great monuments in the history of European architecture; a position for which geographically it only just qualifies, for beyond the hills of Anti-Lebanon which rise above it to the east begin the sands of Asia and an essentially alien mind.

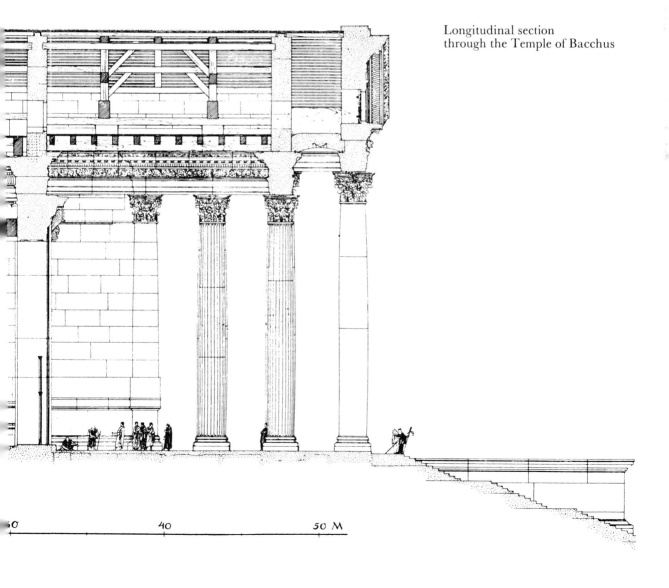

Longitudinal section
through the Temple of Bacchus

50   40   50 M

CHAPTER SIX

The Temple of Venus

Accounts of Early Travellers

A romantic engraving of the Temple of Venus
as seen by Louis Cassas in 1785

JUST as there is a total lack of written Roman sources on the construction of the Temple of Jupiter and the Temple of Bacchus, the same is true with regard to the so-called Temple of Venus.

In fact, the attribution to Venus is debatable, since it is based solely on the decoration of a few external niches which are topped by seashells and which carry doves. But it satisfies the few clues which we do have: first, seashell and dove motifs go well with Venus; second, the multi-curved and delicately carved mass of the temple certainly makes a fitting abode for a goddess; and finally, the hypothetical dedication to Venus conveniently completes the triad of Heliopolitan gods: Jupiter, Mercury and Venus.

THE TEMPLE OF VENUS

Not until the early seventeenth century do we find a specific reference to the round temple. At that time, a certain Franciscus Quaresimus was Apostolic Nuncio in Syria and Mesopotamia. In his *Historica Theologica et Moralis Terrae Sanctae Elucidatio* he rejects the belief of Baalbek's Christian inhabitants: a belief associating the martyrdom of Saint Barbara with the circular temple of the city. We have here an indication that the small temple had already in the 1630s been turned into a church dedicated to Saint Barbara.

That the circular temple was used as a church by the Greek Orthodox of the town is confirmed by Henry Maundrell, who writes in his *Journey from Aleppo to Jerusalem* in 1697:

> Coming near the ruins, the first thing you meet with is a little round pile of building, all of marble. It is encircled with columns of the Corinthian order, very beautiful, which support a cornish that runs all round the structure, of no ordinary state and beauty. This part of it that remains, is at present in a very tottering condition, but yet the Greeks use it for a church; and 'twere well if the danger of its falling, which perpetually threatens, would excite those people to use a little more fervour in their prayers than they generally do; the Greeks being seemingly the most undevout and negligent at their divine service, of any sort of people in the Christian world.

We owe the first exact drawings of the round temple (published in 1757) to Robert Wood. He even provides reconstruction drawings of the round temple, which are remarkably accurate in spite of being prepared back in England, based solely upon sketches made at the site. It is interesting to compare his plan of the Temple of Venus with the one drawn by Krencker about 150 years later. We see the outstanding features of the temple exaggerated, but on the whole the information is correct.

The next important reference to the Temple of Venus is the following comment by Léon de Laborde in 1837:

> At the beginning of our investigations we were led to a small temple built near a brook which later passes along the wall of the castle and turns a mill.
>
> I refer to the drawing by my father which shows the general layout of this small round temple, the search for elegance which distinguishes it, the slightly heavy coquetry which characterizes it. The whole righthand part of the monument, the one which we cannot see on the drawing, has fallen, and the rest will not keep standing for long; the walls are cracking and the columns are out of plumb.

The lithographs of Laborde mirror the romantic mood of the time, as do the enchanting views by David Roberts, who stopped in Baalbek at about the same time. He also describes the round temple in detail and expresses great concern about its future:

53

BAALBEK

About a hundred and fifty yards south-east of the Great Temple stands a detached temple, which must have been one of the most beautiful of those fine buildings in its early day. The entablature and cornice are supported by six columns on projecting bases, like the radii of a circle, forming a grand stylobate, with two columns on each side of the door. A broad flight of steps led to the entrance. The stylobate curves inwards between every two columns, thus forming a graceful corridor. It seems to have been crowned with a cupola, and to have been about twenty-three feet high from the ground. The study of ornament in all these fabrics is remarkable; wherever a wreath, a bust, a statue, could be introduced, it has been placed there. In every interval between the columns, niches have been formed, evidently for statues, for the pedestals remain. The contrast of this temple, in this diminutive size and delicate beauty, with the colossal piles in its neighbourhood, must have been peculiar and striking.

The interior consisted of two stories, the upper surrounded with Corinthian pillars, the lower with Ionic; and in the time of Maundrell it appears to have been used as a church. An exact architectural description of the fabric is given in the folio of Wood and Dawkins, Plates XLII, etc. Dismantled as it is, the eye is instantly captivated by its style. But, a few years will probably level it to the ground. The wild inhabitants have but little value for ruins, beyond their iron and limestone. Earthquakes are continually shaking the soil, and the only hope of saving the last honours of Syria is by rescuing and reviving them in England.

The back elevation of the Temple of Venus in an engraving prepared from a drawing by Borra and published by Wood in 1757

THE TEMPLE OF VENUS

We can see how alarming the state of the ruins must have been, but fortunately no further damage occurred, and when archaeological services were established, the process of natural deterioration was arrested.

The Design of the Temple

Before we begin describing the temple, let us consider the design concept. Circular temples have always been an exception; the rule was the rectangular temple, which in its Roman form rested on a podium. The podium could be ascended only from the front by way of a flight of steps which led into a deep porch or pro-naos. From there, one passed through the large rectangular door into the cella, the rear portion of which was usually raised to form an adytum or holy of holies. The adytum contained the cult statue and clearly constituted the focal point of the whole arrangement. Even if the interior of the cella was lavishly decorated with niches and statuary along the side wall, the pre-eminence of the main god in the adytum was never in question.

In comparison, a circular temple presents many design problems. First comes the definition of an entrance. Basically, a circular temple produces the same elevation in all directions. In order to mark the entrance we have to attach a longitudinal element to the cylindrical body. To the Roman mind this had to be a portico, complete with steps and a podium for the whole temple. When we examine the plan of the Temple of Venus, we see that the porch and stairway take up half the length of the building, the round cella being actually inscribed in the width of the temple. We get the impression that the rear portion of a rectangular temple has been moulded into a curved shape; it seems that the architect wanted to show us the evolution of his thoughts first of all by using a rectangular foundation for the whole building, and then by placing on it a low platform which is rectangular in front, semicircular at the back, and connecting to the first landing of the stairway. That platform conveniently serves as a bench all around the temple. Then comes the podium, already featuring the beautiful curved recesses between the columns all along the round

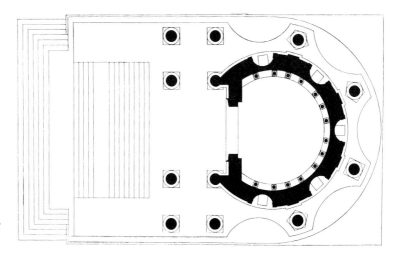

Ground plan of the Temple of Venus

cella which are repeated in the entablature. Situated on top of the platform, the recesses form attractive spaces where half-a-dozen people could gather comfortably for a conversation.

The projections of the podium which remain between the receding concavities serve as pedestals for the columns surrounding the cella. As mentioned earlier, the entablature follows the curvature of the podium, echoing and complementing a rhythmic motion which was introduced mainly to contrast with the convex mass of the cella contained within. The continuous curvature of the cylindrical cella wall is thereby subdivided into clearly differentiated units, framed by pairs of columns. Each unit is further individualized by the presence of a semicircular niche within the depth of the cella wall.

Walking around the outside of the temple, we go past a succession of independent and well-defined exedras, each of which might have been dedicated to a lesser god or goddess, subservient to Venus. If we wonder what kind of statuary had been placed in the external niches, this question becomes even more involved when we consider the interior of the temple. It is lined with two tiers of columns which are spaced in a sequence of one wide and two narrow spaces, with the wide spaces probably designed to contain sculpture. While the lower tier is topped by a continuous entablature, the upper tier carries a succession of circular and triangular pediments. The details of this design are very similar to the architecture of the large temples.

In the absence of an adytum – which is a specifically oriental element – the cult statue must have stood in the middle of the cella, on a simple pedestal centred under the dome above. The figure was not hidden in the dark background of a deep hall, as in the rectangular temples, but rose directly behind the open door, inviting the passers-by to enter and to enjoy the magnificence of the well-illuminated interior.

This disposition is as much opposed in spirit to the concept of the big temples as is the architectural design. Mystical seclusion has given way to joyful openness, overwhelming magnitude is replaced by playfulness in design and detail, turning the temple into a pleasantly human and unconventional masterpiece. For example, the pentagonal Corinthian capitals of the columns around the cella are unique. Their unusual proportions, due to their five-sidedness, are accentuated by a modified arrangement of acanthus leaves. But there is a curious exception: one of the four radial columns has a square capital. This is not the only deviation from strict regularity in the details. There is a certain lack of strictness which is quite typical of the second half of the third century; and we should remember that most of the buildings then under construction in Baalbek were never entirely finished. This trend away from pedantry was probably a prerequisite for the fresh and novel design of the Temple of Venus.

Technically, the construction methods bear all the characteristics of the Baalbek school; one of these is the preference for huge blocks of stone, even when they are structurally unnecessary. In this small temple, stones of 6 to 7 m (20 to 23 ft) in length are common. They were brought to the site in a rough

Three possible reconstructions by Krencker of the front of the Temple of Venus. The one on the right is now regarded as the most likely.

condition, cut to size on the spot, and meticulously fitted together. Sometimes we have the impression that the building was carved out of stone like a piece of sculpture. For instance, the still unfinished rough block for one door jamb is so big that 3 m³ would have to be worked off to reduce it to its proper shape.

Although we can establish the plan and the cella design of the temple perfectly well, the remains of the portico are so limited that no definite reconstruction of the temple front can be presented. The main problem is the large span between the middle columns: 7·28 m (24 ft) are quite difficult to cover by a simple lintel, and buttressing for a false arch would be inadequate. On the basis of scanty evidence, German architects have designed three possible reconstructions: first, with a continuous entablature and a relieving arch contained in the full pediment; secondly, a broken pediment with a lightly recessed segmental vault spanning the central space; and thirdly – the most Baroque approach – two half-pediments projecting right and left from the door, leaving the middle part of the porch open to the sky. This design is probably the one most in tune with the general spirit of the temple, and visitors to Petra will undoubtedly recognize the similarity to the exuberant tomb architecture there.

When the German team began its work, the temple had not been in use for any purpose and was partially covered by houses and gardens. The first step of the temple stairway lay buried beneath 4·80 m (16 ft) of debris. Nevertheless, the small size of the structure – compared with the other enormous temples – made the task of re-establishing its original state relatively easy. The Temple of Venus had not been included in the Arab fortress which incorporated the Temple of Jupiter with its courtyards and the Temple of Bacchus into one solid complex. Instead, it was engulfed by the town, and served as a church for the Christian population.

One important question is the original relationship of the Temple of Venus to the other large temples of Baalbek and to the city. The temple is oriented towards the propylaea of the Temple of Jupiter; but it has recently been discovered that other buildings separated the two. Excavations being carried out by the Lebanese Antiquities Department are slowly revealing the features of the town surrounding the temples and continue to yield many clues to the dedication and exact time of construction of the Temple of Venus. Their findings will be discussed in the general chapter on the town of Baalbek.

The Architectural Significance of the Temple.

When the Romans extended their rule over Hellenic Greece and Asia Minor during the second century B.C., they readily acknowledged the superior quality of Hellenic art and architecture. Greek styles and details were widely adopted in the fine arts, and Roman writers at all times expressed great admiration for the Greek artists. Many even made it their declared aim to adhere faithfully to the principles of the Greek masters. Our knowledge of Greek sculpture rests largely upon the discovery of exact Roman copies; and Vitruvius, our only authentic source on Roman architectural theory, presents the principles of Roman design as a continuation of Greek concepts.

All this led to a widespread belief that Roman art was not much more than an extension of Hellenism. Today our knowledge of Roman art and architecture is so broad that this appraisal has been thoroughly revised. Being no longer limited to the accidental discovery of dispersed antique remnants, we are able to link and compare the buildings of the Roman Empire around the Mediterranean basin with those beyond. Thus, we can discern the changing spirit in which Greek forms were reapplied.

As in other epochs, we witness a movement away from a sober and dry classical approach towards an increasingly free interpretation. But even Roman classicism at the time of the first emperors was as little a direct copy of the Hellenic idiom as was the Renaissance of Italy a lifeless repetition of the classical style.

The new fundamental principles underlying all Roman designs and distinguishing their work from Greek models were twofold:

(1) The imposition of symmetry and axiality on planning; and
(2) The concept of architecture as composition in and with space.

If the Greek approach focused on the artistic placing of beautiful buildings in harmony with the natural environment, the Romans made a superior human order prevail even on difficult and irregular sites. To this end they employed advanced construction techniques, including arcaded and vaulted designs, and used brick and concrete in addition to cut stone masonry. The Greek orders, still used extensively, lost their constructive function and acquired a descriptive significance.

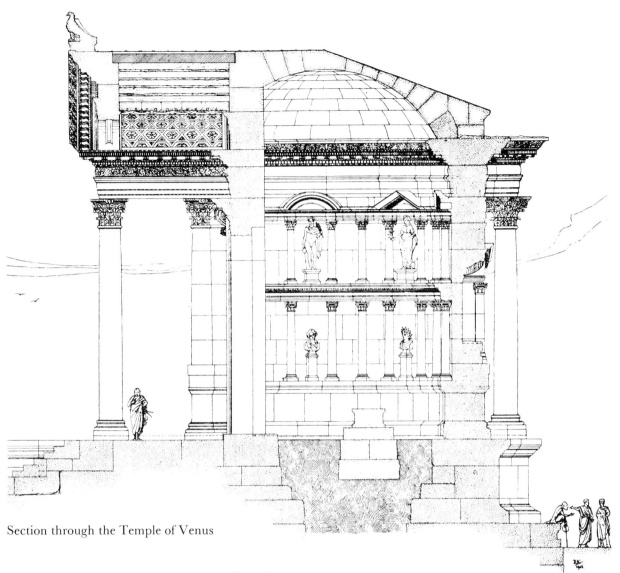

Section through the Temple of Venus

The political stabilization of the Empire under Augustus was accompanied in general by a standardization of forms, an expression of which are the academic treatises of Vitruvius at the end of the first century A.D. Vitruvius was a conservative architect, however, and he does not present a complete picture of the various trends of architecture in his time. Indeed, we can trace back 'progressive' tendencies in decoration to the Ara Pacis in Rome, one of the most important creations of the time of Augustus (11 B.C.). Likewise, the movement towards illusionistic compositions is evident in Pompeiian painting as much as in the three-dimensional treatment of interiors, such as the Temple of Venus in Rome (A.D. 135), the Temple of Diana at Nîmes (c. A.D. 150) or the Temple of Bacchus at Baalbek (c. A.D. 190).

Yet in contrast to the rather rigid temple scheme, the luxurious villas of the Emperors offered almost limitless possibilities for novel departures in architecture. Nero's Domus Aurea in Rome (A.D. 64), and above all Hadrian's villa in Tibur (Tivoli, A.D. 125), are examples of the revolutionary space compositions which the architects of the day were capable of. Particularly characteristic is the contrasting of convex with concave curves, which introduces a pulsating dynamism not present in any previous architecture.

Part of the Villa Hadriana was excavated as early as the beginning of the seventeenth century, and architects like Borromini (1599–1667) or Guarini (1624–1683) derived their inspiration from the Piazza d'Oro and other parts of the villa. If we compare the hall of the Piazza d'Oro with San Carlo alle Quattro Fontane in Rome, and also the small hall of the Villa Hadriana with San Lorenzo in Turin, we see how much this type of architecture is indebted to Roman examples. Violating the rules then acclaimed in academic books on classical architecture, this kind of free design was called 'Baroque' by eighteenth-century classicists, a term derived from the Portuguese word 'barocco' for an irregular pearl. At that time it was a derogatory expression, but today the 'Baroque' quality is esteemed and appreciated in its own right as a concept of art characterized by exuberant decoration, dynamic composition with expansive, curving forms, a sense of plasticity and a preference for spatially complex arrangements.

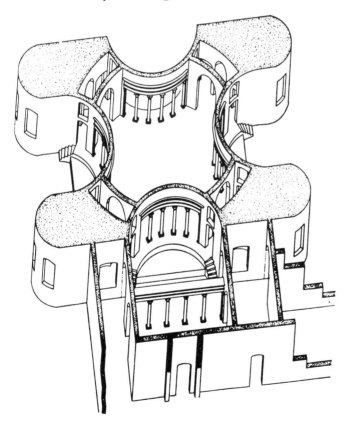

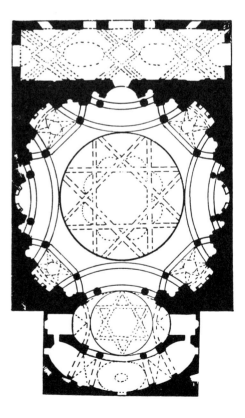

Villa Hadriana, small hall

San Lorenzo, Turin, ground plan

THE TEMPLE OF VENUS

In comparison with the individualistic solution in the imperial residences, religious architecture of Roman times offered very little opportunity for innovation. Under the weight of religious tradition, the Roman temples adhered faithfully to the Greek concept of a rectangular edifice. Yet, even here we find notable exeptions, particularly when the choice fell on circular schemes – the tholos of Greek times. The Temple of Venus in Baalbek is such an exception.

The curved surface of a cylinder immediately suggests movement and spurs the three-dimensional imagination of any designer. Usually the roof of a cylinder is executed as a dome, which is a very distinct space-generating feature. The necessity for thick buttressing walls under the dome requires structural solutions to reduce the mass of the wall without weakening it. The Pantheon in Rome is the supreme example of such economy, achieved through the application of exedras and niches from within and on the outside. In the Pantheon – which is a landmark in the architecture of all times – all attention was focused on its magnificent interior, the exterior being left comparatively plain. Not so in the Temple of Venus at Baalbek. Although it cannot be compared to the Pantheon in size, it shares some key features: a cylindrical cella is joined to a rectangular porch, the wall is reduced to a series of piers by means of niches carved out of it, and the interior is designed in two tiers of aediculae.

The designer of the Temple of Venus had to challenge the grandeur of the immensely larger temples in its vicinity. Furthermore, the Temple of Venus shared a rather small peristylar courtyard with an obliquely placed older temple. Under such conditions the exterior treatment had to offer some special attraction, something hitherto unknown.

The excitingly dynamic design of its exterior, as we still see it today, was an appropriate answer. In a bold and unique composition, the convex body of the cella is hollowed out at intervals by concave semi-domed niches, which are distributed between a peristyle of radially placed columns, carrying an entablature which is neither round and parallel to the cella, nor projecting radially from it, but swinging in and out in a vibrating countermovement; as truly baroque as any creation of the seventeenth century.

This tendency is reflected in the political and religious situation of the same period. After the death of Marcus Aurelius in A.D. 180, the stability of the Roman Empire which had lasted for 200 years was fractured. Men from the eastern provinces such as Syria and Asia Minor rose to important positions, and with them the eastern influence on religion as well as art and architecture became increasingly predominant. The mysterious and the irrational supplanted intellectual reason – an attitude crystallized in Tertullian's dictum on Christianity: 'I believe in it because it is absurd.'

The rear view of the Temple of Venus as
photographed before 1914. The columns are
leaning outwards and are held in place only by the
entablature blocks connecting to the cella.

CHAPTER SEVEN

The Roman Town

SINCE the modern town of Baalbek occupies the same site as its ancient counterpart, archaeological exploration is severely handicapped. It is difficult to justify vast public expenditure for the expropriation of land and the dislocation of people in order to unearth the Roman street pattern and whatever other surprises may lay buried 4 m (13 ft) and more below the present street level. Excavations have recently been extended to areas outside but adjoining the three temples, and they shed new light on their interrelationship. We have learned that the Temple of Bacchus had its own courtyard, and that the Temple of Venus shared one with an older temple, the so-called Temple of the Muses. But the situation is too complex and the evidence too fragmentary to allow any definite pronouncements to be made on the relationship of the temples to the town, or on the town plan itself.

However, we can examine a few individual remains of importance such as other temples, the theatre, the town hall, the fortifications and the necropolis.

1. The Temple of the Muses

This temple, which was discovered during the recent excavations, was of the Corinthian pseudo-peripteral type. It had a porch four columns wide and two columns deep, and six engaged columns on each side of the cella. Professor Kalayan, who directed the excavation, dates the temple at the beginning of the first century A.D.

When the Temple of Venus was built, the level of the courtyard was raised by about two metres, and the podium of the Temple of the Muses, 263 cm (8⅔ ft) high, was for the most part buried. The name was chosen because of an inscription on the south side of the podium of the Venus Temple. This inscription relates that on the first of September in the Seleucian year 742 (A.D. 430) the very admirable Lupus, one of the citizens of Baalbek, had paid for the construction of underground drainage channels in this area, to protect the enclosure of 'The Muses'.

2. The Temple of Mercury

An important temple, which has practically vanished today, was the one built on Sheikh Abdallah hill, south of the town. The main indication of its previous existence is a monumental flight of stairs cut out of the rock of the hill, 10 to 12 m (33–39 ft) wide. Fragments found in the vicinity included parts of engaged half-columns and brief inscriptions referring to Mercury, but the clues to the identification of the temple are coins struck by Philip the Arab, which show a

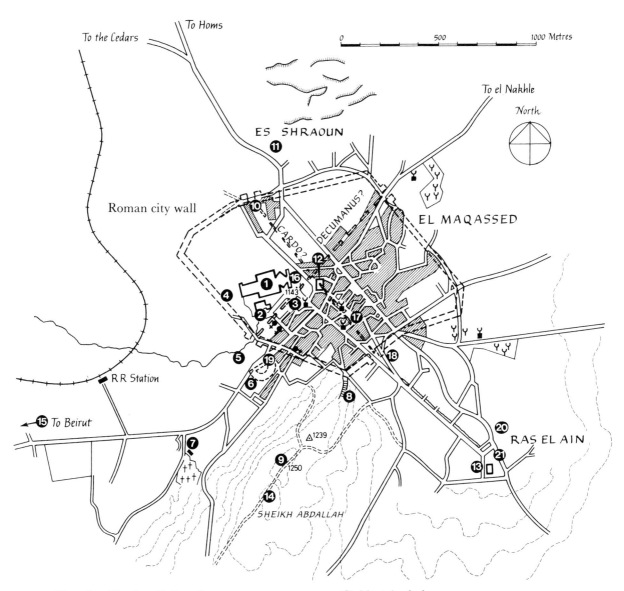

To the Cedars

To Homs

To el Nakhle

North

ES SHRAOUN

EL MAQASSED

Roman city wall

DECUMANUS?

CARDO?

1143

RR Station

To Beirut

1239

1250

SHEIKH ABDALLAH

RAS EL AIN

1 Temple of Jupiter Heliopolitan
2 Temple of Bacchus
3 Temple of Venus
4 Trilithon
5 Colonnade of a public building
6 Theatre (not excavated)
7 'Stone of the Pregnant Woman'
8 Stairs to the Temple of Mercury
9 Site of the Temple of Mercury
10 Roman city gate
11 Necropolis
12 Great Mosque
Built on the site of the Roman Forum, it dates from
the Umayyad period and consists of three rows of
columns carrying arches on which a wooden roof
once rested. The irregular granite and limestone
columns with their Corinthian capitals were taken
from the Roman temples. In the north-west corner
of the courtyard there are traces of an octagonal
minaret placed on a square base.
13 Ruined Mosque

14 Qubbat Amjad.
On the top of Sheikh Abdallah hill are the remains
of a mausoleum ascribed to Al Amjad Barhan Shah,
grand nephew of Saladin. It is built of stones from
the Temple of Mercury.
15 Qubbat Douris
On the outskirts of Baalbek, on the west side of the
main road, are the remains of a simple octagonal
mausoleum. It consists of eight red granite column
shafts, taken from Baalbek and used as simple
pillars without base or capital. Over the architrave
blocks is a remarkably designed frieze, cut in such a
way as to relieve the architrave of any additional
weight. The monument was built in the thirteenth
century. Nothing of the domed roof remains.
16 Tourist Bureau
17 District Government
18 Post Office
19 Hotel Palmyra
20 Hotel Khawam
21 Restaurant Ras el Ain

stately pseudo-peripteros on a mountain, with a distinct stairway leading up to it. Included in it is a caduceus, the insignia of Mercury.

3. The Theatre
At the foot of the same hill was the theatre of Baalbek. Today the Palmyra Hotel partially covers it and no excavations have been undertaken.

4. The Town Hall
Across the street from the Palmyra Hotel a large area has been cleared and lofty colonnades have been rebuilt by the Lebanese Department of Antiquities. They are believed to belong to a group of public administration buildings, including a bouleuterion or town hall.

5. The Fortifications
The ancient fortifications surrounded the whole town except for the theatre, which the Romans uncharacteristically built outside the town walls. Starting from the acropolis, the wall roughly prescribed a pentagon with side lengths of 500 to 700 m (1600 to 2300 ft). The wall was generally 2·70 m (9 ft) thick, with square towers projecting at about 30 m (100 ft) from each other. There were four gates defining two axes across the town, which are nearly at right angles to each other. They intersect at the compound of the old mosque which has been built over the Roman forum.

Of the gates, only the one to the north-west escaped total destruction and that because part of it was incorporated in barracks built by Ibrahim Pasha. Enough remained, though, to allow a pictorial reconstruction by the German team.

6. The Necropolis
Just as the cliffs around the town have long been quarried for the enormous amounts of building material needed for construction, so they have been pierced and carved by people in search of tombs that would last. Doubtless many an abandoned quarry became a graveyard later on. Not only did cutting tombs in the rock satisfy the desire for permanence but also the fertile plains were too precious to be used as cemeteries. There are basically three types of rock-cut tombs at Baalbek: the simple shaft tomb, barely large enough to receive the coffin; the plain tomb chamber which was supposed to accomodate a few sarcophagi; and the elaborate vault with recessed burial chambers and entrance lobby.

No remarkable finds can be reported from any of these tombs since they were all robbed well before the appearance of an archaeologist.

A reconstruction of the Roman north gate

Opposite, the mosaic floor of the dining room of the House of Patricius

7. *The House of Patricius*

Given the pleasant climate, the abundant water supply and the attraction as a religious centre, ancient Baalbek also became a residential town housing many well-to-do and literate citizens. The House of Patricius, which was discovered on the road to Ras el Ain, and in particular the magnificent mosaics which adorned the floors of this villa, eloquently demonstrate the sophisticated taste of the time. Being very well preserved, the mosaics were dated to the fourth century A.D. and have been transferred to the Beirut National Museum.

The finest design was on the dining-room floor and consists of a large circle within a square which is further subdivided into eight circles arranged around a central figure of Calliope, the Muse of eloquence and poetry. In the eight circles around her are depicted Socrates and the Seven Sages. Every medallion carries in Greek letters the name and origin of the philosopher shown and gives one of his famous sayings, such as 'Know thyself' for Chilon of Sparta; 'Recognize opportunity' for Pittakos of Lesbos; 'Reflexion hastens work' for Periander of Corinth; 'Moderation is best' for Cleobolus of Lindos; 'Most men are wicked' for Bias of Priene; 'Caution attracts ruin' for Thales of Miletus; and

66

'Nothing in excess' for Solon of Athens. Other scenes in adjacent rooms show Alexander the Great and his parents, representations of Summer and Earth and, fortunately, inscriptions revealing the name of the builder of the house and the name of the artist, a certain Amphion.

CHAPTER EIGHT

Byzantine and Arab Baalbek

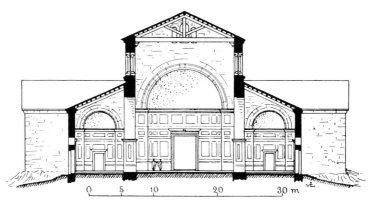

Above and opposite, reconstruction drawings of the Christian basilica

The Byzantine Period

T HE temples of Baalbek were built in a pure stone masonry technique, almost entirely without the use of mortar. It is evident that this work was time consuming. In order to accelerate construction, all work was put up in a rough state, the finishing of the visible surfaces being done later on the building itself. Consequently, when Emperor Constantine in A.D. 313 declared Christianity the official religion of the Roman state, work was still going on towards the completion of many embellishments, in spite of the fact that the sanctuaries had been in use for generations. Constantine's decision probably brought the work to an abrupt halt, but it did not put an end to pagan worship.

According to Paschal the Chronicler (A.D. 610–641), Constantine contented himself with closing the temples of the pagans, and Eusebius of Caesarea (A.D. 260–340) commends the Emperor for building a church in Heliopolis. At times Christian fanatics tried to stop pagan worship, and we read of Rabbula, later bishop of Edessa, going to Baalbek, city of the heathen, accompanied by Eusebius, to destroy the idols in the temples. However, they almost suffered martyrdom by being beaten unconscious and thrown down the huge flight of stairs.

Julian, the successor of Constantine, reverted to paganism, destroyed the church at Baalbek, and persecuted the Christians in Syria. Lack of accurate, unbiased written sources makes it difficult to give a clear picture of the following years, but pagan ritual seems to have continued until Theodosius (A.D.

68

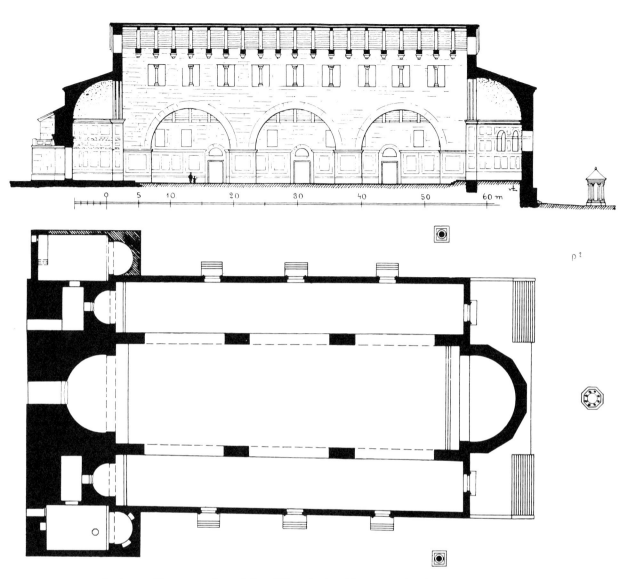

379–395). According to a chronicler, Theodosius 'destroys the famous trilithon, sanctuary of Balanios and turns it into a church'. What he actually did was to tear down the altar and the tower in the Great Court and build a stately basilica in their place, re-using their material. This procedure of tearing down and building anew was typical in the Orient, where the conversion of temples into churches, which frequently took place in the west, was not regarded as sufficient.

The Basilica, dedicated to St. Peter, measured 63 by 36 m (207 by 118 ft), and consisted of a nave and two aisles, each separated by three large arches. The building was raised 2 m (6 ft) above the court level, in a fashion which

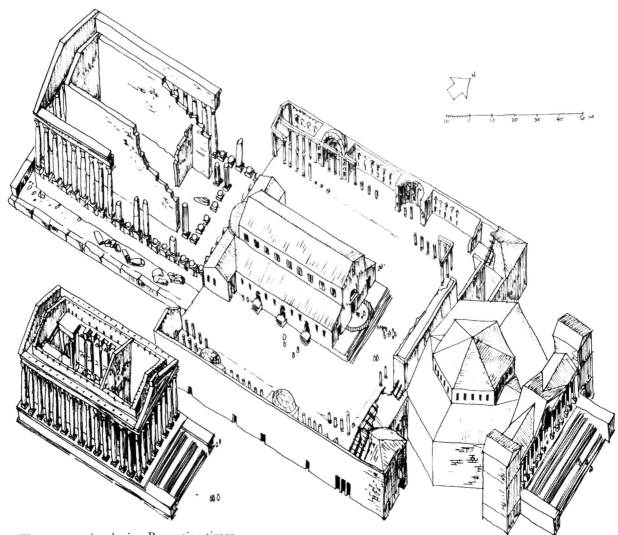

The sanctuaries during Byzantine times.
A large basilica, dedicated to St Peter, stands in the
Great Court. The plan shows the original arrangement
with the entrance from the east. The Hexagonal Court
features its legendary roof. Roman construction is partly
destroyed, partly decaying. The ancient timber roofs
have collapsed exposing the substructures of stone.

meant that the three apses at the west end cut into the upper portion of the
stairway to the Temple of Jupiter, with a wide flight of steps leading up to the
entrance at the east.

It is difficult to say how much was left of the Temple of Jupiter at this stage.
In the absence of gunpowder or dynamite the destruction of such a mighty

structure was no simple matter. The debris covering the Great Court and raising the Basilica above its level was composed of material from the Temple of Jupiter as well as the colonnade surrounding the Great Court. Stones from the upper parts of the buildings were found lowest down, proving the systematic process of destruction. Most thoroughly destroyed were the countless sculptures of major and minor gods and goddesses, of emperors and generals, which adorned the courtyards. Liquidation of these symbols of heathen times was so complete that no sculpture to speak of has ever been found in Baalbek.

Not long after the construction of the Basilica, the increasing pressure of orthodox Christian rules necessitated the reversal of its plan. Although access to the court had to remain from the east, the entrance to the church was shifted to the west by removing the original apses and cutting away at the temple's stairs. In this way a new apse could be built at the east end of the church, as prescribed by the new tradition. At the same time a baptistry was added.

According to tradition, the Christian builders, being occupied above all with the creation of interior spaces, even covered the Hexagonal Court. Considering the clear span of 37 m (121 ft) this was probably done in wood, creating a pyramidal form.

By now the Acropolis had been turned into a Christian sanctuary, but this did not mean that all the population had become Christians. There seems to have been a continuing co-existence between Christianity and paganism. Baalbek is repeatedly cited by Christian writers as a centre of heathenism. Michael the Syrian declares that a temple in Heliopolis was struck by lightning and burnt down with its idol inside. The dimensions given of the building fit precisely the Temple of Bacchus, and the story seems to indicate that at this time the Bacchus cult was still alive. Theophanes writes of a persecution under Justinian, affecting the people in Heliopolis, and John of Ephesus says that in the year A.D. 579 the ruling class in Heliopolis was heathen.

Under Emperor Tiberios I Constantinos a punitive expedition managed to extract information of a secret heathen organization covering Heliopolis, Antioch and Edessa. The ensuing prosecution possibly crushed the remaining pockets of paganism. By that time the Acropolis had been freely used as a quarry of ready-made masonry blocks. Fortunately, most of the construction was so gigantic that it withstood the pillage. It is said that some of the most valuable columns of red Aswan granite which surrounded the courtyards were transferred by Justinian for use in the building of the church of Haghia Sophia.

Arab Baalbek

Whatever the progress of Christianity, it turned out to be shortlived. By the seventh century, Byzantium and Persia were exhausted from endless fights for hegemony in the Near East. From A.D. 611 to 622 Syria was a Persian satrapy, but once more Heraclius, the Byzantine Emperor, restored his rule over the region in six successive campaigns (A.D. 622–629). Then, a few years later, an entirely unexpected and overwhelming power entered the scene: the Muslim Arabs.

> In the name of Allah the merciful! This is a statement of security for the inhabitants of Baalbek, the Byzantines, Persians and Arabs living there, safeguarding their lives, their property, their churches, their houses within Baalbek and outside, and their mills. The Byzantines may graze their cattle up to 15 miles from the town, provided they do not exploit already settled places; when the months Rabi' and Jumâda I have passed, they may move wherever they please and those who adopt Islam shall have the same rights and obligations as we do. The merchants of Baalbek may travel to any country which has made peace with us. And those of them who stay shall pay head-and-property tax. May Allah witness this and be sufficient as witness.

Such were the words of a charter issued by Abu Obaida, the general of Khalid ibn al-Walid, the conqueror of Damascus. They were addressed to the inhabitants of Baalbek in the year A.D. 637, and under such generous conditions the city entered the Islamic period. The decree offered the inhabitants three possibilities: to emigrate, to adopt Islam and become equal with the ruling Arabs, or to stay without changing one's religion while paying a poll and land tax. Several months were allowed for deliberation, during which time the Byzantines were permitted to use the pastures in the vicinity. For generations insecurity and heavy taxes had made life difficult. Maybe the new rulers would at long last bring peace and security? To the autochthonous Semitic population, the invaders must have been closer in kin than the Byzantine or Persian overlords, and it is an indication of the survival of pre-Roman traditions that, with the establishment of Arab rule, the original name Baalbek begins to reappear in the annals. Furthermore, the habit of the early Arab rulers of residing outside populated areas, in splendid desert castles, eliminated unnecessary friction. All this may explain the speed of the Arabization that took place in the years that followed.

Arab writers such as Baladhuri and Ibn Qalanisi give us detailed accounts of the succession of rather turbulent events during early Arab times. Baalbek was generally dependent on Damascus. In A.D. 662 difficulties seem to have arisen in Baalbek because Caliph Muawiya I moved some of the Persian inhabitants to the coast and to Cyprus, bringing in turn people from Samaria to settle in the town.

In the middle of the eighth century Umayyad rule in Damascus declined and power shifted to the Abbassid court in Baghdad. Baalbek found itself at the fringe of Muslim held territory and became the target of Byzantine incursions. Not until the tenth century under Fatimid rule was security again established, but then in 1075 the Seldjuks put an end to Fatimid domination.

The Umayyad
mosque

 During this time the Crusaders entered the Syrian coastland, and it is indicative of the political situation that the local Seldjuk governor of Baalbek immediately plotted with the Franks to move against Sultan Toghtikin residing at Damascus. In the twelfth century Zengi, the ruler of Aleppo, planned to conquer southern Syria. He did not succeed in taking Damascus and instead captured Baalbek in the autumn of 1139.

73

By that time, the Temple of Jupiter had been turned into a citadel, which held out for two months against Zengi's attacks. Finally, the defenders capitulated on condition that they were given free conduct and no harm was done to the inhabitants. However, Zengi massacred the surrendering garrison and carried many men and women into serfdom. His treachery outraged his contemporaries, and all writers of the period condemned his violation of a pledge, given solemnly on the Koran.

Zengi appointed Saladin's father, Najm al-Din Ayyub, governor of Baalbek, and in the years that followed he did not cease in his attempts to gain control of Damascus. Onor, the defender of the town, was finally forced to call the Franks to his aid, and they agreed to start a campaign in the Hauran. In gratitude Onor conquered Banias for the Crusaders.

Zengi retained control of Baalbek till his death in 1146. There are three stones in the north-western Tower of the Kala'a, carrying Kufic inscriptions

Opposite, the interior of the Arab fortification tower

Section through the Arab fortification wall and view of the fortress tower built on the steps of the Temple of Bacchus. (The upper part of the tower no longer exists.)

referring to Zengi as 'Imad al-Din' (pillar of Islam), protector of the world, friend of the caliphate, subjugator of the non-believers, etc.

Onor regained Baalbek without difficulty, but he died three years later, and in 1153 Nur-al-Din, the son of Zengi, took over the city. He not only improved the fortress of Baalbek but, according to an inscription, also furnished the town with a wall.

Much of this work was severely damaged by the disastrous earthquake of 1170, but repairs were immediately carried out. Although these measures were mainly designed to strengthen his position among the Arabs, Nur-al-Din also championed the Moslem cause against the Crusaders, who were far from defeated. Once during Nur-al-Din's time Christian prisoners escaped and took refuge in the citadel of Baalbek. However, pursuing Moslems gained access through a secret hole in the wall and killed the Franks.

With Nur-al-Din's death in 1174, a new man came to power who was destined to end the Crusaders' fortunes in the Holy Land: Salah-al-Din, commonly known as Saladin. He gave Baalbek, which had always been a coveted possession, to a succession of deserving followers, among them Izz al-Din Farrukhshah, his first general, who had defeated the Crusaders at Kerak. Izz al-Din's son inherited Baalbek and ruled it from 1182 till 1230. He extended the fortification, two towers of which bear inscriptions to this effect (south-west corner). He also built a small mosque on Sheikh Abdallah mountain.

After Saladin's death in 1193, the Crusaders and Moslems reached an agreement which led to a partitioning of Palestine. Saladin's territory was parcelled out among his sons, inviting subsequent quarelling.

Finally around 1250 a group of Circassian, Turkish and Mongol army officers seized power in Egypt. They founded the so-called Mamluke (literally 'slave') dynasty. They were destined to rule till the advent of the Ottoman Turks, and their first great foes were the Mongols under Hulagu, grandson of Jenghis Khan.

In January 1260, Hulagu's general Ketbogha swiftly conquered Aleppo, Damascus and Baalbek, spreading death and destruction wherever he went. Fortunately, in the August of the same year Sultan Qotuz of Egypt defeated the Mongols decisively at Ain Djalut and expelled them from Syria.

On his triumphal return from the victory over the Mongols, Qotuz was assassinated by his rival Baibars, who ascended the throne. He and his successor Qalaun fully consolidated Mamluke domination and expelled the remaining Franks. They engaged in a systematic construction programme of strategic fortifications and brought about the last radical changes in the Acropolis of Baalbek.

What place lent itself better to transformation into a fortress than the Acropolis of Baalbek? Situated high above the surrounding terrain, either on podiums impossible to scale or enclosed by smooth thick walls, it took relatively little effort to turn it into an imposing stronghold.

In the wake of the Mongol invasion, Baibars repaired the citadel of Baalbek as well as the town and quartered a strong garrison in it. Qalaun further improved the fortifications of Baalbek and also renovated the main mosque of the town. His eldest son Khalil (1290–1293), who is commemorated as victor over the Crusaders and 'subduer of the servants of the cross', did not content himself with using only the Temple of Jupiter and its courts, but included the well-preserved Temple of Bacchus by extending a high wall from the south-west corner of the Great Court across to the south-east corner of the temple, strengthening this exposed spot by a mighty fortification tower. New fortifications were added to the west of the Temple of Bacchus, creating a large court to the south of the Temple of Jupiter. Construction included a mosque, baths, living quarters and cisterns. The huge vaults below the Acropolis furnished ideal storage facilities. A new intricate entrance with all the latest defence techniques was created at the south-west corner of the complex, while the propylaea of the Acropolis were totally changed. The stairway, almost 50 m

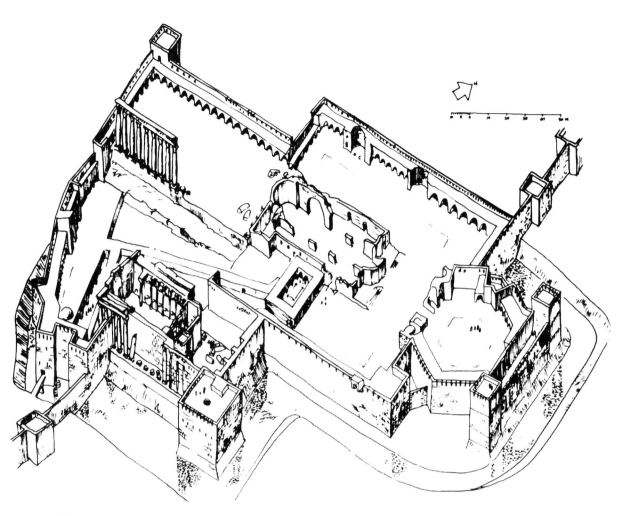

The Arab Fortress.
The Acropolis and the Temple of Bacchus have
been turned into a huge fortress surrounded by a
moat. The moat was later filled by material
dumped during excavation of the ruins.
Connecting to the fortress are the city walls. The
basilica is shown in ruins although it was used as
a palace for some time.

(165 ft) wide, was removed and the material used to fill the spaces between the columns of the portico. External decorations were cut off to render the walls unscalable, and finally Sultan Barquq (1382–1393) added a deep moat, to be filled with water, all around the fortress. Like the Propylaea, all temple peristyles facing the outside of the complex were closed – a procedure which actually contributed to their preservation. All along the perimeter casemates were constructed, using pointed vaults topped with mud bricks. The tops of these vaults served as platforms for the defenders who operated behind a chain of battlements. Naturally, all these changes were made without the least regard for the classical buildings. While dismantling old masonry during the Middle Ages, workmen must have been delighted to find strong metal clamps, dowels and lead at every joint. Consequently, it became a pastime to chisel into joints to recover the precious metal. Thereby the excellently conceived structures of interlocking masonry were unwittingly reduced to gigantic sets of dominoes, liable to slide and fall at the slightest tremor of the earth.

Also during the Mamluke period, the colonnade of the main mosque was repaired and a new mosque at Ras al-Ain was built. In addition, a mausoleum built for Yesheh, the governor of Damascus, who died at a battle near Baalbek, is worth mentioning. The invasion of the Tartars under Timurlane around 1400 left Baalbek untouched.

In 1517 Baalbek became part of the Ottoman Empire and ceased to play any role beyond its local limits. The fortress was abandoned. In some parts, villagers moved in and built their simple houses in the shelter of the mighty walls. Sand and earth were allowed to collect gradually, walls and columns continued to tumble, vegetation started to grow, and in 1759 another severe earthquake reduced the standing columns of the Temple of Jupiter from nine to the present six.

Until 1857 the town was in constant decline under the irresponsible rule of the local Harfush dynasty. Most travellers complain about the lack of hospitality at Baalbek and the many acts of vandalism committed to the monuments. Sometimes the authorities took drastic action, as related by the Frenchman, Dr. Granger, in 1735:

> Baalbek is a small town built of the rubble and upon the ruins of a very old city which according to the best historians was Heliopolis. Recently it was governed by an Emir, but a year ago, the Grand Seigneur had the Emir's head cut off and dispatched a governor with the title of Pasha to replace him, with two hundred soldiers under his command.

Volney in 1784 has the following to say:

> The condition of the town is not less deplorable than that of the monuments. The bad government of the Emirs of the Harfouche Clan had already been disastrous, and the earthquake of 1759 ruined

it completely. The wars of the Emirs Yousef and Jessar have further aggravated the situation: of 5000 inhabitants who were counted in 1751, only 1200 are left, all poor, without industry and commerce and without any other crops than some cotton, maize and water melon. In the whole area the ground is meagre and continues to be such, both up to the north and down to the south-east towards Damascus.

About forty years later de Laborde tells us:

Baalbek is the capital of the prince of the Metvalis. This little chief pays tribute to the Pasha of Damascus; but he is even more dependent on the prince of the mountains. He calls himself El Emir Amin, and he lives at the moment in his country house, six leagues from Baalbek. His absence exempts us from a reception, and what's more, an ennui.

Commenting on the economic conditions he remarks:

One half of the population is Metvali, the other Greek Catholic, but altogether it is so small in number, and so enervated that the Maronites of Lebanon come to cultivate the lands of Baalbek. In order to protect them in their work, the Emir Beshir keeps one of his officers with the Emir of the Metvalis.

CHAPTER NINE

The Rediscovery of Baalbek

As the veil of Ottoman domination descended on Baalbek and the city fell into the lazy sleep of decadence, a new era had begun in the West, prompting men in search of knowledge to visit the famed remnants of ancient history in the Near East. We can hardly imagine today how long and hazardous such a journey was. Each of these travellers made his contribution to learning, though their writings are occasionally faulty or naive. But these people had little to guide them: they had no tools but their inquisitive minds and their open eyes. When they returned home they wrote books about what they had seen so that others might share in their wonder. A book on Baalbek would be incomplete without an account of their findings and impressions, which are our only sources of information on the fate of the monuments up to the end of the nineteenth century.

The first travellers whose records still exist did not recognize that the Arabic citadel had huge Roman temples at its origin. Thus Benjamin of Tudela who visited Baalbek around 1170 talks of a palace, and above all is impressed by the huge stones of the Trilithon and the absence of any mortar between them. More than three hundred years later in 1492 Bertrandon de la Brocquière only observes the town and a castle.

Sixteen years later the Austrian knight Martin Baumgarten, after the early loss of his wife and child, sought consolation by travelling to the Orient. On 13 January, 1508, he came to 'Baldach', as he calls the place, and continued his journey on the 16th. He admired the rows of columns incorporated into the castle, the huge stones, and the towering structures, and concluded that they must have been of great importance. In his diary, however, the funny story of how the big stone in the western quarry came to be known as the 'stone of the pregnant woman' occupies much more space than the sentence describing the ruins. His diary was not published until 1594 in Nuremburg and so the first travelogue to be issued was written by Pierre Belon who visited the site forty years after Baumgarten but published his 'Observations' in 1553.

The thirty-year-old French physician writes about 'the antiquities of the town of Caesarea, now called Balbec', and like many an earnest visitor today, he complains that 'a man interested in antiquities cannot see everything there is in Balbec in eight days, because there are many old things and most impressive ones which are beyond my description; also we did not stay there long'. As we shall see later, Belon was criticized for his lack of details.

About the same time André Thevet, 'Cosmographe du Roys', must have been there. Baalbek is mentioned in his *Cosmographie Universelle*, Paris 1575. He

The nine columns of the Temple of Jupiter
as seen by Robert Wood in 1751

tells us of having seen 27 columns of different heights, some of which were taken by Suleyman the Magnificent to Constantinople for the construction of his mosque (1550–1556). Since the highest columns in this mosque are only 9 m (30 ft) high, they cannot have been from the temples but rather from the great courtyard of the Temple of Jupiter. Otherwise Thevet speaks only in general terms of 'plusieurs antiquitez' and of cut stones unusually huge, which he has not even seen himself but heard local people talk about.

Prince Nicolas Christopher Radzivil visited Baalbek on 13 and 14 June 1583, on a pilgrimage to Jerusalem in fulfilment of a vow. He came from faraway Lithuania and wrote his story in Polish, having it translated into Latin and published in Braunsberg in 1601. He subscribes to the local tradition, according to which the ruins are those of the Palace of King Solomon in the Lebanon (I Kings 7, 2–7) by stating:

> This however I can confirm without doubt; I was able to establish by thorough and careful study that this same place is described in the Book of Kings exactly as it can be seen in Baalbek until today. This can be comprehended even more fully, since the palace was not destroyed unto its foundations, but had been used since time immemorial as a quarry before finally collapsing.

He rejects absolutely Belon's theory concerning Caesarea Philippi.

The question concerning the relationship of the ruins to the palace of Solomon is also of great importance to our next visitor, Franciscus Quaresimus, Apostolic Nuncio for Syria and Mesopotamia. For ten years he travelled widely through Syria and in 1639 he published a *Historica Theologica et Moralis Terrae Sanctae Elucidatio*. He firmly rejects any identification of the ruins with Solomon's palace, as well as with Caesarea Philippi and above all with Nicomedia, the last stemming from the assumption of the local inhabitants, who linked the martyrdom of Saint Barbara with her worship in the round temple of Baalbek. Quaresimus turns out to be a very keen observer because he recognizes the ruins from their style and the Latin inscriptions as Roman. He even accords the big temple to Jupiter and admires the sculptured ceiling of the peristyle in the small temple. He also mentions the biggest stone of the trilithon, stating its length to be 20 m (66 ft), and he counts 55 columns remaining – which must have been the total number in all the temples.

Still more exact, and for a long time to come the best description, is that produced by a gentleman from Lyon who studied at the University of Salamanca and became 'Conseiller due Roys'. Balthazar Monconys loved travel, and from 20 to 23 December, 1647, he visited Baalbek. While filled with admiration, he views the ruins with strict objectivity and correctly grasps the site in its entirety and structure. Although he does not realize its meaning, believing the Heliopolitanum to be a palace, he recognizes correctly the entrance from the east through the propylaea, despite the still existing Arab enclosure. He regards the smaller temple as a building apart from the others, observes the raised altar in the interior and mentions the sculpturing of the lintel, which however he considers to be one piece, thus proving that the sliding down of the key-stone cannot have begun at that time. He even describes in a few words the relief depicting a sacrifice in the lower part of the pronaos wall. Monconys not only takes some measurements in the ruins of Baalbek, but also makes two rather simple sketches which are included in the text and have to be regarded as the first illustration of Baalbek. The strength and correctness of his observations are nowhere better illustrated than in the strenuous efforts he made to read and understand inscriptions:

> The 23rd (December) I revisited the palace and for a quarter piaster
> I had one of the bases of the columns in front cleaned and I could
> read clearly in the first line M.V.M.DIIS. HELIPOL. PROSUL.

He thereby confirms on the spot the identification of Baalbek with Heliopolis, verifying the view of Postellus, a French Orientalist who travelled through the East in the sixteenth century, collecting rare manuscripts.

Twenty years later, the French minister Colbert started an organized search for coins, manuscripts and antiquities in general. To this end he sent three men to the Orient between 1667 and 1675. One of these, Monsieur de Monceaux, is of interest to us. He visited Baalbek in 1668 and two years later, back in France, he started to write his travelogue. In a note to Colbert, he requested access to the library of the King, and Colbert allowed him to take two books at a time. Unfortunately, no copy of de Monceaux's work is left, but reference to it is found in Fréret's fifth volume of the *Voyages de Corneille Le Bruyn*, published fifty years later. Monceaux also seems to have made a number of drawings, which were rather distortedly turned into fifteen engravings by the Parisian architect Jean Marot. Montfaucon's *Antiquité Expliquée* uses them and Claude Perrault, the architect of the Colonnade of the Louvre, refers to them.

Our next visitor, Jean de la Roque, is also familiar with the texts and plates of de Monceaux, so much so in fact that he is later accused of having copied from them. Having descended with Father Clermont and de la Tuillerie from the Cedars on 31 October, 1689, he claims to have enjoyed the sheikh's hospitality:

> The ruler of Baalbek was not a common sheikh; he was a man of
> merits and not superstitious . . . he liked explorers and scientists, and
> thought quite differently from those who believe that the Franks are
> only treasure hunting in the ruins.

The travellers were put up in the serail:

> the term serail is no exaggeration, because the sheikh made a palace
> out of an ordinary house, not sparing the ruins of ancient buildings,
> neither the marbles nor all the other ornaments with which he used to
> accommodate himself magnificently at the expense of antiquity.

BAALBEK

Before their departure, 'the sheikh asked what we thought of all the great buildings which we examined with so much curiosity, and why people do not build this way any more. He appeared satisfied with our answers, and talked further about the fortunes of the Arts which have had, he said, an ancient origin and which were brought to perfection after much progress, and later unreasonably declined in decadence; but, like all other human things, the Arts can re-establish themselves again in time, provided that the masters of the world endeavour to favour them.'

Describing the ruins, the author makes a point of discrediting Pierre Belon, of whom he says: '. . . although his book carries the name *Observations*, he observed almost nothing in this place'. He stresses also the identification of Baalbek with Heliopolis and criticizes the ignorance of the inhabitants of the town, who only tell fables of demons or believe that Solomon built the majestic monuments. Finally, he passes to a more wordly subject, without however revealing his own impressions: 'One reads in the anonymous Greek geographer who lived under the empire of Constantine . . . that anciently the most beautiful women in Asia were to be found in this town . . . such suns of beauty that one would say Venus had established her court at Heliopolis and there distributed the charms of beauty. Besides, the town of Heliopolis produced musicians and instrumentalists of the first order, the excellence of whose art was particularly inspired by the Muses of Lebanon.'

The first traveller to write in English whose account we can quote was an English chaplain in Aleppo. Coming from Damascus on the way to the Cedars, Henry Maundrell and fourteen of his compatriots arrived at Baalbek on 5 May, 1697, to spend not more than a day there.

> Wednesday, 5 May . . . At Baalbek we pitch'd at a place less than half a mile distant from the town, eastward, near a plentiful and delicious fountain, which grows immediately into a brook; and running down to Baalbek, adds no small pleasure and convenience to the place.
>
> In the afternoon we walked out to see the city. But we thought first, before we enter'd, to get license of the governor, and to proceed with all caution. Being taught this necessary care by the example of some worthy English gentlemen of our factory, who visiting this place in the year 1689, in their return from Jerusalem, and suspecting no mischief, were basely intrigu'd by the people here, and forc'd to redeem their lives at a great sum of money.
>
> Baalbek is suppos'd to be the ancient Heliopolis, or City of the Sun, for that the word imports. Its present Arab, which is perhaps its most ancient name, inclines to the same importance. For Baal, tho' it imports all idols in general, of whatsoever sex or condition, yet it is very often appropriated to the sun, the sovereign idol of this country. The city enjoys a most delightful and commodious situation on the

east side of the valley of Bocat (Beqa'a). It is of a square figure, compass'd with a tolerable good wall, in which are towers all round at equal distances. It extends as far as I could guess by the eye, about two furlongs on a side. Its houses within are all of the meanest structure, such as are usually seen in Turkish villages.

At the south west side of the city is a noble ruin, being the only curiosity for which this place is wont to be visited. It was anciently a heathen temple, together with some other edifices belonging to it, all truly magnificent: but in later times these ancient structures have been patch'd and piec'd up with several other buildings, converting the whole into a castle, under which name it goes at this day. The adjectitious buildings are of no mean architecture, but yet easily distinguishable from what is more ancient.

This is followed by his remarks on the Temple of Venus which have already been quoted in Chapter Six, p. 53. He then describes the Temple of Bacchus, observing details such as

... The portico is cover'd with large stones hollow'd arch-wise, extending between the columns and the wall of the temple. In the centre of each stone is carv'd the figure of some one or other of the heathen gods, or goddesses, or heroes. I remember amongst the rest a Ganymede, and the eagle flying away with him, so lively done, that it excellently represented the sense of that verse in Martial, Illaesum timidis unguibus haesit onus.

He describes the doorway of the temple in detail and then offers the following observations of the interior:

About eight yards distant from the upper end of the temple, stands part of two fine channell'd pillars; which seem to have made a partition in that place, and to have supported a canopy over the throne of the chief idol, whose station appears to have been in a large niche at this end. On that part of the partition which remains, are to be seen carvings in relievo, representing Neptune, tritons, fishes, sea-gods, Arion and his dolphin, and other marine figures. The covering of the whole fabrick is totally broken down, but yet this I must say of the whole, as it now stands, that it strikes the mind with an air of greatness beyond any thing that I ever saw before, and is an eminent proof of the magnificence of the ancient architecture.

Maundrell correctly assesses the remaining columns of the Temple of Jupiter by saying:

About fifty yards distant from the temple, is a row of Corinthian pillars, very great and lofty; with a most stately architrave and cornish at top. This speaks itself to have been part of some very august

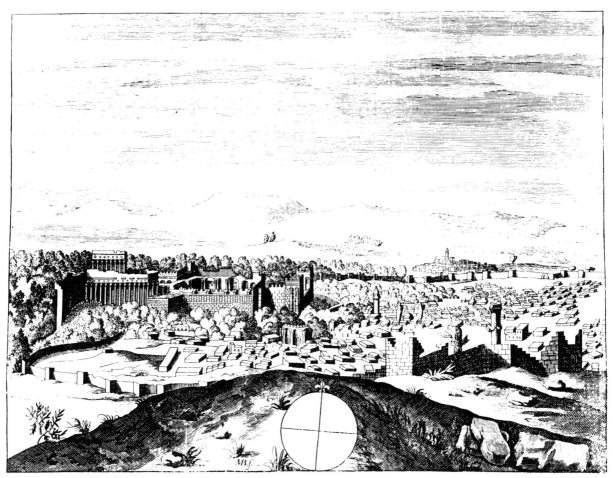
Baalbek as seen by Henry Maundrell in 1697

pile, but what one now sees of it is but just enough to give a regret, that there should be no more of it remaining.

When writing about the trilithon he is worried that he will not be taken seriously:

Here is another curiosity of this place, which a man had need be well assur'd of his credit, before he ventures to relate, lest he should be thought to strain the privilege of a traveller too far. That which I mean is a large piece of the old wall, or peribole, which encompass'd all these structures last described. A wall made of such monstrous great stones, that the natives hereabouts (as is usual in things of this strange nature) ascribe it to the architecture of the devil. Three of the stones, which were larger than the rest, we took the pains to measure,

86

and found them to extend sixty one yards in length; one twenty one, the other two each twenty yards. In deepness they were four yards each, and in breadth of the same dimension. These three stones lay in one and the same row, end to end. The rest of the wall was made also of great stones, but none, I think, so great as these. That which added to the wonder was, that these stones were lifted up into the wall, more than twenty foot from the ground.

In his illustrations, Maundrell conceives impressive if wrong reconstructions of the Temple of Bacchus in its details, based upon contemporary notions of Roman architecture. His most original contribution is the first general view of Baalbek as seen from Sheikh Abdallah mountain. All in all an admirable amount of material for a day's visit.

In 1745, *A description of the East and some other countries* by Richard Pococke was published in London. It contains eleven engravings of Baalbek, based upon his observations on the spot from 15 to 21 June, 1737. Unbelievably inaccurate and unreliable, they do not merit much attention. Anyway, twelve years after their appearance they were overshadowed by Wood's great book *The Ruins of Balbec, otherwise Heliopolis in Coelesyria*.

Filled with the highest spirit of the Society of Dilettanti – admission to which they hoped to gain through their travels – the wealthy English amateurs John Bouverie, James Dawkins and Robert Wood set out from Rome in 1750 on a voyage to Asia Minor. After Bouverie's death in Magnesia, his two companions went on to Athens in the spring of 1751, where they met two friends, the English painters Stuart and Revett. Partly financed by Dawkins, these two had explored the Greek antiquities and now joined the party on their journey to Syria, accompanied by an assistant, the Italian architect Borra. In his introduction to his book on Palmyra, Wood describes their way of travelling and working.

After having worked for fifteen days in the desert city, they arrived in Baalbek on 1 April, 1751. Well organized as they were, Dawkins and Wood produced truly scientific work. The book on Baalbek, a big volume with 46 illustrations and 28 pages of text, does not offer detailed descriptions, because the editor wants the reader to study the plates instead. Where deemed necessary, a few matter-of-fact remarks are added. For the first time there are drawings of the round temple and the architecture of the courtyards, and in the small temple the foremost line of columns is revealed. The illustrations depict the condition of the ruins generally in perspective and give a realistic impression of their appearance. There are also reconstructed plans, elevations and sections of whole buildings, or parts thereof, but these are not without errors in the details, which is understandable since they were completed at home.

Dawkins and Wood did not excavate anything but restricted their work to the description of structures that were still visible. This explains their biggest

87

Overleaf, a view from the Hexagonal Court to the remaining columns of the Temple of Jupiter. In the background, left, a part of the Temple of Bacchus. From Robert Wood's treatise of 1757.

mistake: missing the colonnades that once surrounded the two courtyards of the acropolis. In the introduction they try for the first time to determine the exact age of the buildings and arrive at the conclusion, still uncontested, that there is no reason to doubt the report by John Malalas that the temples had been built under Antoninus Pius.

Thirty years later, Volney, the next distinguished visitor to the site, wrote about their work:

> One cannot add anything to the fidelity of the description by these travellers; however, since their presence some changes have taken place: for instance, they found nine great columns standing, while I in 1784 found only six ... It's the earthquake of 1759 which caused their fall.

In contrast to the well-organized voyage of the rich Englishmen – who after their return were duly accepted as members of the Society of Dilettanti – Constantin-François Volney set out alone from his home town, with a haversack on his back, a gun on his shoulder, and 600 livres in gold hidden in his belt. About 25 years of age, he took his legacy on foot to Marseilles, from where he sailed to Egypt, '... without any other motive than to use the time of a restless youth for procuring knowledge of a new kind'. For eight months he studied Arabic in a Coptic monastery; then in 1784 he visited Baalbek, and in 1787 his travelogue was published – rapid results, indeed.

His well-organized, concise and clear description, systematically accompanied by illustrations, was very popular with travellers of later years, and John-Lewis Burckhardt wrote upon his visit on 29 September, 1810:

> After the work of Wood and the account of Volney it is completely superfluous to describe these ruins.

As an example of a less fortunate person in matters of publication, one may cite the case of Louis François Cassas, a French painter specializing in landscapes and architecture. In the course of his journey through Syria, Palestine and Egypt he came to Baalbek only one year after Volney. His sketches and watercolour paintings are of much higher artistic value than those by any of his predecessors. He exhibited a selection of them in Rome in 1787, arousing Goethe's highest admiration. Cassas planned a monumental work of some 330 plates, and publication was started with private financing. It was later taken over by the government of the French Republic, but of the fifty plates planned on Baalbek only fourteen were published. With few exceptions, they rank with those by Wood in archaeological accuracy, and even surpass them in one or two instances. The entablature of the big Temple, parts of which had fallen down during the earthquake of 1759, was now easier to examine and Cassas depicted it more correctly. Had his work been finished, it would have surpassed that by Wood; incomplete, it could hardly influence the literature of coming years.

With the beginning of the nineteenth century, romanticism became the guiding influence on world travellers. Their imagination was spurred by the beautiful publications of the archaeological pioneers; they no longer saw a need for careful recording but rather wanted to fulfil their romantic visions. At their best they were artists or poets creating rapturous or melancholy images of great attraction, but their contribution to scientific understanding is small.

Typical of this attitude is that of the young Léon de Laborde who, accompanied by his father, stayed in Baalbek from 21 to 23 March, 1827. He wrote:

> It takes more talent and strength to reconstruct a ruin than to build a monument; only nature is permitted to touch at ruins, she frames them with verdure, shades them with beautiful trees; their moss and their thorns are welcome.

Then he continued:

> The view of these magnificent monuments gives me a violent urge to draw, and strong desire to put on paper the remembrance of my impressions; nevertheless, it is more reasonable first to see everything in order to grasp the general disposition of this grand ensemble . . .

Having done so, he commented:

> One could speak of monuments made in Rome, labelled, packed and forwarded to here like a jigsaw puzzle.

Father and son made sketches which served as models for picturesque lithographs later published in their book of travels. With artistic licence they sometimes misrepresented reality; for instance, on one page the southern half of the great court has been omitted to allow a view of the round temple in the background.

Another visitor in the romantic vein is Lamartine, who as a poet is very frank about his predilection. He was in Baalbek in March 1833, and his accounts of it are a string of totally superficial and fleeting impressions. Upon approaching the ruins he said:

> We shall not formulate any theory regarding the totality of the ruins we resign ourselves to looking at them and admiring them without understanding anything but the colossal power of human genius and the force of religious ideas which could move such masses and accomplish masterpieces like these.

In imagination, Lamartine even outdid the Arabs, who thought the huge stones had been moved by demons under Solomon's order; he suggested that they were proof of human power at the time of Noah or even before.

A year and a half later, on 3 September, 1834, another sentimental traveller arrived in Baalbek. He was Marshal Marmont, once Duke of Ragusa. Although deprived of his title and undertaking a voyage of consolation, he seems to have enjoyed comfortable circumstances:

My caravan was composed of twenty-three horses, thirteen of which carried our baggage. I was equipped with three tents, one for me, one for my companions and the last for my servants, and all necessary camping utensils. I had added a certain number of Arab helpers to my French servants. Everyday we camped near a fountain at a chosen site, and to the end of my voyage, I did not fail to lead a way of life which recalled the one of my good years.

Fortunately, in his report he simply reproduces Volney's description. This is a welcome modesty, for his own observations may best be judged by his description of the round temple (omitted by Volney), which he considers more ancient and more tasteful than the big temple:

It is formed of a double arch of triumph with four doors and recalls the temple of Janus at Rome.

The most accomplished painter to visit Baalbek was without doubt David Roberts. The number and the artistic quality of sketches he produced during his grand tour of the Near East are astonishing. He arrived at artistically superb compositions by freely adding or omitting elements in his pictures, and he usually succeeded in expressing forcefully the special character of each monument. Faced with the splendours of Baalbek, however, he admits:

I feel that it must be difficult to convey, even with the pencil, any idea of the magnificence of this ruin, the beauty of its form, the exquisite richness of its ornament, or the vast magnitude of its dimensions.

Indeed in his limited number of Baalbek views he employs the monuments as a romantic backdrop, in front of which he arranges exquisite scenes of oriental life with richly dressed ladies and gentlemen, serenely lounging in an idealized setting. This, of course, gives a false picture of the true condition of the place at the time, but his lithographs are still treasured for their exquisite beauty.

As the number of enthusiastic amateur visitors increased, flowery reports of their impressions abounded. Particularly popular became moon-light visits to the site, because 'by the uncertain light which reigns at this hour, the greater part of the deficiences are supplied by fancy, and the mind is irresistibly carried back to the period of their perfect state'. More and more we witness the emergence of the upper class tourist who travels for the sake of romantic pleasure and exotic adventure rather than intellectual edification.

A contrasting and decidedly more modern type of traveller is the thrifty, sporting character, who sets out with an open mind and looks at everything with unashamed enjoyment. One such traveller, who surprisingly enough travelled alone in the 1860s, was an anonymous lady, C.G.; she was dressed in a cool summer riding habit of brown Holland, a light Leghorn hat with a broad brim, and a yard or two of white muslin wound round it, with long ends

The Temple of Bacchus and
Arab fortifications from the east

to protect her head and neck from the sun. She had not forgotten her nice little spirit lamp, with the equipment for making tea, and she took along some preserves, sardines, biscuits and boiled eggs. She was honest enough to write in her *Extracts from My Journal in Syria* that finally 'the columns of Baalbek came into view at a considerable distance, and appeared to be quite small. I felt a little disappointed, and ready to exclaim "Can this be Baalbek, the most imposing structure of Syria?"'. Very appropriately she continued:

> The fact is that the exquisite proportions of the columns give them the aspect of such airy lightness, even at a little distance, that one can scarcely credit their vast magnitude till actually standing beside them. Then indeed . . . the mind is overwhelmed by the view, and words can hardly express its feelings of admiration and wonder.

The only visitor to make substantial new discoveries during the middle of the nineteenth century was Louis Félicien de Saulcy, who visited Baalbek from 16 to 18 March, 1851. For the first time he recognized the Christian church built in the large courtyard and identified it with the one mentioned in Theodosius' *Chronica Paschalis*. He also thought the exciting podium walls of the Temple of Jupiter to be remains of a pre-Roman temple. Furthermore, he examined the city wall, climbed Sheikh Abdallah hill, and in his report he mentions several little things which have vanished since.

With the French intervention in Lebanon, the country and its sights were made fully accessible to the West: a road was built from Beirut to Damascus, and at the end of the century Baalbek became a stop on the railway to Homs.

Ernest Renan was entrusted with the archaeological exploration of the region occupied by French troops. He represented the new species of scientist to whom Roman work was too recent to be of real interest. When he visited Baalbek it was rather to satisfy himself that pre-Roman remains did not exist there, although he considered the possibility that the huge stones of the Trilithon were of Phoenician origin – not because of their gigantic size which in itself cannot prove extraordinary age, but because he saw no inherent relation between the Roman temple and this work.

In 1890 the first modern-style tourist guide was published by Michel Alouf: *A History of Baalbek by one of its Inhabitants.* Answering a growing need, it was translated into several languages and continually revised. It is still found in bookshops today.

A new page in the history of Baalbek was opened at the turn of the century when it received its first imperial visitors.

Towards the evening of 10 November, 1898, the German Emperor Wilhelm II and his wife arrived by carriage at their destination. Near the end of a long journey through Palestine, their guide, Professor Moritz of Cairo, insisted upon a visit to Baalbek. The tent encampment was prepared in the Great Court. On the morning of the 11th a memorial plaque donated by the Sultan was unveiled with great ceremony. Shortly after 8 a.m. the party continued its journey. It was a brief visit, but what the Emperor had seen was enough to make him decide upon the need for a thorough exploration of the site. This decision sparked the first professional excavation at Baalbek.

As we have seen, previous archaeological accounts were the product of a rather romantic search for the marvels of the past and especially the renowned splendours of the east. They remain to this day fine examples of architectural reporting, although they cannot claim a high degree of accuracy. The destruction wrought by the centuries, the large number of alterations and additions made in post-Roman eras, as well as the tremendous extent of the ruins made a completely accurate tracing of the original scheme quite impossible.

In view of the technical difficulties, it is understandable that until the end of the nineteenth century the ruins of Baalbek not only remained untouched by the archaeologist's shovel, but were also subjected to the unchecked rigours of a climate which brings snow and frost in winter and searing heat in summer. It must be regarded as a sheer stroke of luck that the famous six columns of the Temple of Jupiter have survived upright till our time, when modern techniques could assure their future existence.

The initiative of the German Emperor put to work the wealth and knowledge of a nation which had a prestigious record of archaeological discovery and therefore all essential qualifications for a successful excavation of the Temples of Baalbek.

Only one month after his visit, the Emperor ordered the distinguished archaeologist Koldewey, who was about to leave with his colleague Andrae for Babylon, to survey the ruins of Baalbek in preparation for the campaign. A fortnight later Koldewey, Andrae and Professor Moritz arrived on the site and carried out their investigations in snowy and cold weather.

After a month the group produced an elaborate report containing a number of drawings, illustrating the amount of rubble which needed to be removed before definite results could be obtained. Koldewey suggested the clearing of the antique structures down to the former floors, excavations to the foundations, possibly to discover remains of pre-Roman times, and also some conservation work. He correctly anticipated that no remarkable statuary or inscriptions would be found since the ruins had undergone too many changes in the Byzantine and Arab periods.

The project, which Koldewey calculated would last for four years, was approved by Wilhelm II, and the Prussian Ministry of Culture was entrusted with the execution. It toook more than a year of preparation before a new team of specialists settled down in Periklis Mimikakis' Hotel de Palmyre at Baalbek.

The scientific archaeological exploration of a site resembles very much the investigations of a team of detectives on the scene of a crime. In this instance, there was, first of all, the team of investigators which included a variety of specialists: Professor Otto Puchstein, an archaeologist and the director of the group; Bruno Schulz and Daniel Krencker, two architects; the Arabist Moritz

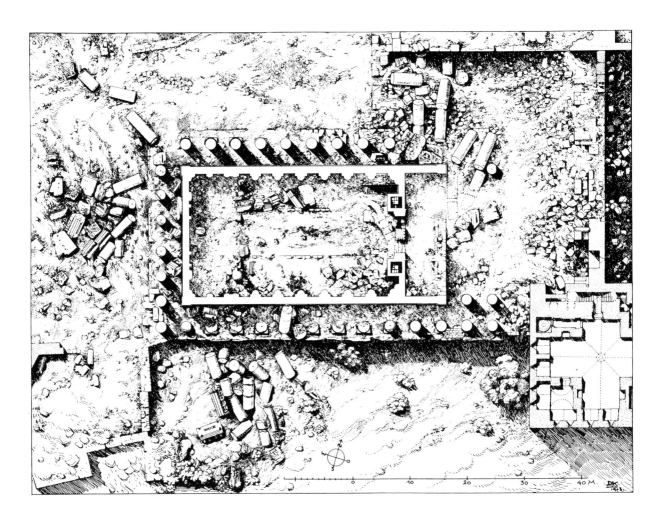

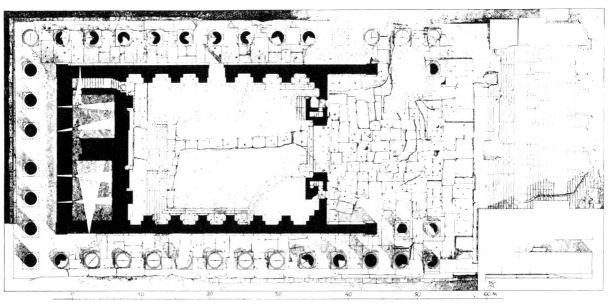

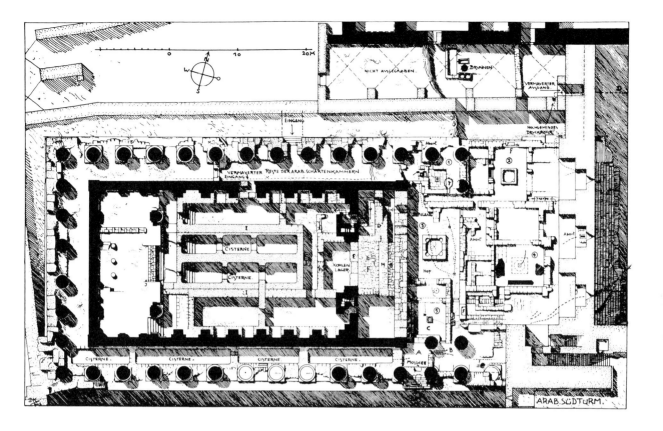

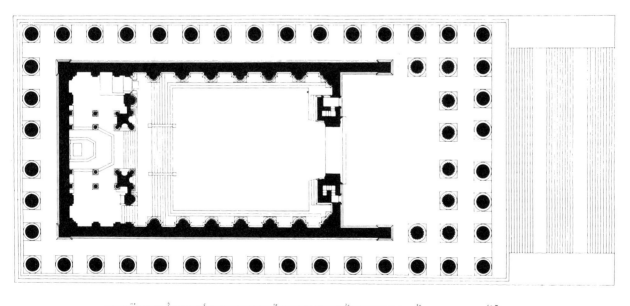

Drawings from the German archaeological expedition showing, *above left*, the condition of the Temple of Bacchus before the excavations of 1900, *above right*, Roman and Arab remains after removal of the rubble, *below left*, Roman remains after removal of Arab additions and, *below right*, a reconstruction of the original Roman condition.

Sobernheim, and the photographer Meydenbauer; and Makridi Bey as representative of the Ottoman government.

Excavation started in September 1900 and was essentially completed after two years. At times the work force numbered 150 men, and the operations were facilitated by a field railway. Land had to be acquired in certain areas before excavations could proceed.

From the outset a high standard of performance was established, without regard to increased expenses. No stone was to be touched before its location was recorded; no late construction interfering with the original Roman work was to be removed before its significance had been fully studied; no excavation material was to be dumped where it might have spoiled the final appearance of the ruins.

Most of the Arab moat was filled, thus restoring the ancient relationship between the sanctuary and the surrounding land. Stones of no artistic value were sold to the inhabitants of Baalbek by the Turkish government and removed from the site by the buyers.

In 1902 the German Consul Luetticke put his villa at Ras el Ain at the disposal of the expedition, and its headquarters were moved there. This improvement not only meant more comfort for the scientific team but certainly saved them from being affected by the cholera epidemic in 1903 and the smallpox infection in the following year. At the same time Heinrich Kohl, a construction supervisor, joined the group.

Apart from the preparation of painstaking written and drawn records, extensive use of photography was made to catalogue the overwhelming amount of details coming to light. Nearly 300 pictures were taken, 138 of the above involving plates of 40 by 40 cm (16 by 16 in). At the same time photogrammetric methods were employed to facilitate later preparation of scale drawings. As the criminologist collects all possible evidence for the eventual solution of a crime, so the archaeologist takes note of all details which may assist him in the reconstruction of a building.

As an example, let us study the successive steps taken in the excavation of the Temple of Bacchus.

First, the original condition of the site at the arrival of the expedition was charted.

Second, all rubble was removed and the construction of the various periods was identified.

Third, all later additions were eliminated, and a plan showing the Roman ruins in their present condition was prepared.

Fourth, based upon the available evidence, a plan of the Temple in its original condition was drawn.

To this we have to add the study of the elevations and sections of the building, involving countless details of architectural, historical or technical significance. Twice during the campaign, members of the team led by Puchstein visited related Roman sites in Syria. These comparative studies in the region were necessary for the overall understanding of the monuments in Baalbek and resulted in the later publication of an independent volume on the Roman temples in Syria.

By the end of March 1904, the work on the site was practically completed. As a finishing touch, part of the stairway in front of the propylaea was rebuilt to facilitate access by tourists – it is still in use today. While the party was returning home, Berlin requested permission from Constantinople to acquire a number of architectural samples. Not until a year and a half had passed was this permission granted, and finally in November 1905, 57 crates were shipped from Beirut.

The evaluation of the findings, including thorough research on historical sources, comparison of art forms, detailed reconstructions, preparation of elegant presentation drawings and perspectives, and the formulation of final scientific conclusions constituted a project in itself. It necessitated repeated site checks to clarify open questions. Unfortunately Otto Puchstein died in 1911 and other participants were killed in the war. Two new men, Theodor Wiegand and Karl Wulzinger, were commissioned to complete the work, and it is quite amazing to hear that as late in World War I as 1917 they not only travelled from Germany to Baalbek but even persuaded the German Military Detachment in Damascus to use a warplane for aerial photography.

The publication of the painstaking work was undertaken with an artistic flair quite rare today in an age of dry scientific evaluation. However, the result of the war impeded and greatly delayed the final presentation. The number of illustrations had to be reduced, paper quality was poor, and few volumes found their way beyond the limits of Germany.

CHAPTER TEN

How the Temples were Built

PROBABLY the most impressive aspect of the Roman sanctuaries at Baalbek is the extraordinary boldness of their conception. What immense self-confidence, what faith in the immortality of the Roman empire must have been required for people to engage in projects which they knew would take several generations to achieve. Not only did they plan on a vast scale, they also chose to continue the classical technique of solid masonry construction, partly in recognition of a deeply rooted local tradition, partly in consequence of their conservative attitude towards religious architecture. As we shall see, the observance of local stone masonry traditions brought about some remarkable solutions, but let us first review a few of the basic planning principles.

The Orientation of the Temples

At the outset of an undertaking as important as, say, the Temple of Jupiter, serious thought must have been given to its orientation. Yet the question of a temple's orientation is a perplexing one because many factors have to be taken into account, such as the topography of the site, existing buildings and traffic patterns, local traditions, religious beliefs and astronomical relationships.

Vitruvius, our Roman source, tells us in his *Fourth Book on Architecture*, Chapter V, how the Temples should be oriented:

> The quarter toward which temples of the immortal Gods ought to face is to be determined on the principle that, if there is no reason to hinder and the choice is free, the temple and the statue placed in the cellar should face the western quarter of the sky. This will enable those who approach the altar with offerings or sacrifices to face the direction of the sunrise in facing the statue in the temple, and thus those who are undertaking vows look toward the quarter from which the sun comes forth, and likewise the statues themselves appear to be coming forth out of the east to look upon them as they pray and sacrifice.
>
> But if the nature of the site is such as to forbid this, then the principle of determining the quarter should be changed, so that the widest possible view of the city may be had from the sanctuaries of the gods.

HOW THE TEMPLES WERE BUILT

In Baalbek, the direction of the main axis of the acropolis seems to have been established during pre-Roman times, as recent excavations in the courtyard indicate. The Temple of Jupiter faces a direction 76° 09′ east from north, or about 14° north from east. This corresponds to the preferred Greek practice of holding ceremonies in front of the east end of the temple in the morning. A study by the author revealed that the statue inside the adytum will have received the direct light of the rising sun through the open door from mid-May till mid-June, and from the end of August to the end of September. It is quite possible that these early morning illuminations were the highlight of a pilgrimage, but when we remember that worship took place in front of and below the temple, near the altar, nobody could actually have seen the god's image. The only place from which it could have been seen clearly was the platform of the tower behind the altar. This interplay of effects must have made a most powerful impression.

The Temple of Bacchus is oriented in the same way as its greater companion, while the Temple of Venus turns towards the common space in front of all three Temples.

Proportion

It is well known that classical design is based upon a system of proportional relationships embodied in formal orders of architecture. The orders we are familiar with have been established in retrospect, mostly by Renaissance architects, who surveyed classical buildings and derived from them their own definition of ideal proportions. The Greeks, who developed the Doric, Ionic and Corinthian orders, did not repeat two buildings in exactly the same proportions but kept evolving from heavy beginnings to more graceful and lofty solutions. The Romans, inheriting the Greek formulae, were more pragmatic and tried to lay down definite canons for design, adding the Tuscan and Composite orders in the process.

Generally the system of proportions is related to the diameter of the bottom of the column shaft, half of which is called a module. The module is further sub-divided into thirty units or parts. The size of every part of a structure is then expressed as a multiple or fraction of the module, and as soon as the actual dimension of one element is decided all the other dimensions are determined.

Thus we may choose the height of a façade and, given a certain order, we can automatically deduce the thickness of the columns and their spacing. Although this formalism facilitates the job of the architect to the point of design-mechanization, it embodies the danger of freezing architecture into a set of lifeless rules.

How far modular design was applied to complete elevations and to plans is a matter of dispute. There seems to have been a relationship between the length and the width of a temple; and usually the number of columns on the long side is equal to twice the number of columns on the short side plus one.

Again the only classical source of information available to us is the famous *Ten Books on Architecture* by Vitruvius (1st century B.C.). He obtains his *modulus* for temples by dividing the breadth of the stylobate into a certain number of equal parts, but he also states that the difficult problems of symmetry and proportion are solved by geometrical rules and methods (III–IV 3).

Although the Romans used the foot as the linear unit of measurement 29·7 cm ($11\frac{3}{4}$ in) the great importance which was attached to geometric relationships in the field of design does suggest that sequences of measurements were derived from geometric construction rather than linear layoff. The most famous of such designs is the 'golden section', which is derived from the side relationships of a right-angled triangle, producing the pleasing sub-division of a line into two parts in which the shorter part relates to the longer part as the longer part relates to the whole. The proportions between sides and diagonals of squares were particularly popular and they were often developed in sequences. Drawing a square the side length of which is unity, we obtain $\sqrt{2}$ times unity as the diagonal. Drawing a rectangle with $\sqrt{2}$ times unity as base and unity as height we obtain $\sqrt{3}$ times unity as diagonal. Continuing in the same fashion we can produce a series of lengths which are the products of unity times the square roots of whole numbers. This kind of relation was called a dynamic progression.

Professor Kalayan has found markings of small squares measuring 51·44 cm, which is 29·7 times square root 3, and he is inclined to believe that classical proportions were more a question of involved geometric rules than the application of simple arithmetic multiples of a given unit such as the modulus. He found that, except for the horizontal measures, all vertical dimensions are a multiple of square root 2 and square root 3, with a margin of error of less than one per cent.

Scale

Whatever the principles of geometric layout and proportioning were, the weakness of classical design at overblown dimensions is its lack of human scale. In this respect it was a self-defeating undertaking to build taller and larger without changing the vocabulary of forms, because there is no reference from which the observer can derive the actual size of a part. And it is meaningless to take a picture of the six solitary columns of the Temple of Jupiter without including a known object such as a human being for scale reference.

Yet, in the complete condition we can see how effectively the architects preserved the monumentality of their designs. They accomplished this by means usually associated with Late Renaissance architecture. Let us take as an

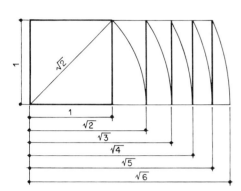

Geometric derivation of the
square roots of whole numbers

Detail of the interior elevation of
the Temple of Bacchus

example the interior of the Temple of Bacchus. The walls are vigorously articulated by projecting columns on pedestals. The columns span the full height of the space and are actually continued up to the roof truss by the use of a broken entablature which at the same time eliminates the dominance of a continuous horizontal superstructure. The walls in between carry two tiers of *aediculae*, that is, applied arches or pediments which rest on colonettes. In the spaces thus created there will have been statues which must have been very close to natural size. Since scale can only be grasped by comparison with familiar elements, the observer could identify himself with the statue, from which he could judge the size of the aedicula and finally appreciate the magnitude of the columns and the whole space. The effect being similar to the use of the Giant Order, introduced by Michelangelo one and a half millennia later.

The full impact of the grandiose setting would have been felt in ceremonies involving vast crowds of people, similar to that which we can experience in St. Peter's Square in Rome. Indeed, it is most revealing to compare the monuments of Baalbek with other familiar works of architecture and to ponder the different size impressions. The Parthenon in Athens is smaller than either the Temple of Jupiter or the Temple of Bacchus, but, astonishingly, the Pantheon in Rome would span right over the Temple of Bacchus; St. Peter's Basilica would easily contain the Temple of Jupiter, while the Pyramid of Cheops would cover them all.

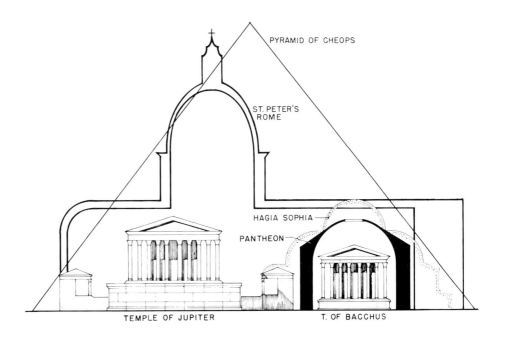

Structural Design

Let us now consider the excecution of the work. The Romans were fully aware of the importance of perfect foundations for the lasting stability of a building. They knew from the start what tremendous weights they would pile upon each other, and therefore they decided correctly that nothing but solid bedrock would be sufficient to serve as a footing. This meant, in the case of the Temple of Bacchus, that in places the foundation had to extend down to 17 m (56 ft) below ground level – the equivalent of five modern basement floors. The excavation and shoring of the retained earth therefore represented a difficult task in itself. Later civilizations were much more negligent in this respect, relying on optimistic assumptions rather than complete certainty. As a result of Roman precaution, the masonry remaining in place has not settled a single millimetre. In fact, if one were to check a modern water level for its accuracy one could confidently use the horizontal joints of Baalbek as a gauge.

The masonry construction did not rely on mortar as a cementing agent, but was composed of perfectly cut stones placed one upon the other and hooked together by iron or bronze clamps and dowels embedded in lead. This rendered the whole structure quite elastic, like a system of massive beads of a necklace, all linked together. Such a structure was able to ride out earthquakes with surprisingly little damage. Nevertheless, earthquakes contributed most to the destruction of the temples, not, however, without the initial help of man. When the temples ceased to be used for worship and became dead remnants of a bygone age, people discovered the treasures of metal concealed in the masonry and relentlessly chiselled away at every promising joint to retrieve it. Thus, paradoxically, the very measure which was taken to ensure the stability of the structure contributed essentially to its destruction. Iron and bronze were well coated with lead to avoid any oxidation with concomitant increase in volume, which would have resulted in cracking of the stones. Disregard of this technique by other people, as in the reconstruction of several European cathedrals, produced devastating effects.

Iron clamps were also used to reinforce weak stones. On the ground between the Temple of Bacchus and the Temple of Jupiter we can see a cornice block mended in this way. The outer surface of the metal is corroding but the inner sides with their coating of lead are safe and still serve the purpose they were meant for.

From the structural point of view the greatest problems were posed by slender, freestanding features such as columns, and above all by spanning parts such as lintels, beams and roofs. When we examine the remnants of the temples with this in mind, we can only marvel at how much the builders knew about the strength of materials and the laws of statics.

The Temple of Jupiter has a total height of nearly 48 m (157 ft) from the ground to the top of the cornice: the podium is 12 m (39 ft) high, the stylobate 2 m

(6 ft) and the temple itself 23·8 m (78 ft). The temple in turn consists of 20 m (66 ft) columns and a 3·8 m (12 ft) high entablature. It might be worth mentioning here that the Temple of Bacchus is only about ten per cent lower, its columns for instance measuring 17·6 m (58 ft). The main difference is in the height of the podium, which is 'merely' 5·20 m (17 ft) in the Temple of Bacchus.

Let us now examine the colonnade of the Temple of Jupiter in more detail. The columns are composed of a 1 m (3 ft) high base, a 16·6 m (54 ft) high shaft and a 2 m (6 ft) high capital. The only taller columns from antiquity in existence today are those of the great Hypostyle Hall of the Temple of Amon at Karnak in Egypt. But those columns were built out of many blocks of stone and to a much heavier proportion. The shaft of a column of the Temple of Jupiter consists of only three pieces, the longest, which is roughly 7 m (23 ft), being at the bottom. Recent studies of column fragments spread around the temple even indicate that the corner columns were monolithic – for reasons which we shall discuss below. Such a shaft would have weighed about 130 tons.

The clear span of the architrave between the capitals is a modest 1·5 m (5 ft), but the weight piled on top is enormous. The slightest imbalance could have been disastrous. Great pains were therefore taken to centre the loads upon the columns. The entablature consists of two rows of blocks only, the lower row combining architrave and frieze, the upper row forming the cornice. The lower blocks have lap-joints in order to strengthen the bond. The cornice blocks are cut in a special way. Centred over each column is a block with stepped vertical joints so that the single central block, which is itself stepped, will not load the middle of the architrave but rest on the two adjoining stones. To ensure the desired bridging effect, the horizontal joint below the filler piece is left with a small clearance.

As well as achieving in this way a good central loading of the columns (which reduced the danger of buckling), the builders further increased the stability of the structure by carefully fixing the columns themselves. The base blocks extend a full 1·20 m (4 ft) below the finished floor surface and the column drums received three dowels at each joint. All this work was done with roughly cut blocks with up to 10 cm (4 in) extra surface thickness for finishing at a later stage.

In order to prevent damage to projecting edges such as the ends of column shafts, these parts were made non-bearing by means of receding profiles or slight undercutting. Thus, all projections were protected from the risk of being chipped as a result of oscillations.

In other structures, as in the Temple of Bacchus, there is only one dowel in the middle of each column joint. A small channel was cut in the upper surface of each drum, and the next drum was lowered into place with the dowel embedded and projecting. The final connection was made by pouring molten lead through the channel to the dowel. However in the case of the huge blocks at Baalbek the lead would have solidified before reaching the dowel. Probably in this instance subsequent blocks of stone with the dowels fixed on their under-

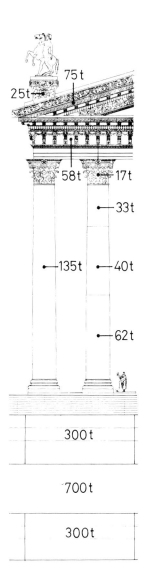

25t
75t
58t — 17t
— 33t
—135t — 40t
— 62t
300t
700t
300t

Left, approximate weights of the
construction elements of the
Temple of Jupiter and, below,
details of the connection between
the shaft and base of columns.

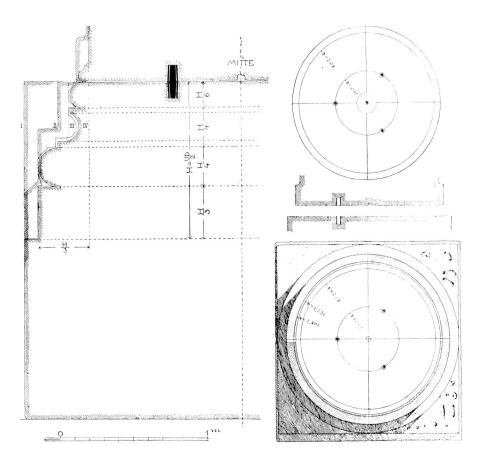

side were lowered into pre-leaded holes, the tremendous pressure of the load
displacing the soft metal and achieving a firm connection.

The greatest loads on the columns occur under the pediments, which are
designed as solid stone walls. At the Temple of Jupiter the pediment attains a
height of 11·50 m (38 ft) in the middle, where it carried a huge quadriga on
top. The raking cornice over the pediment (e.g. the inclined cornice) was also
constructed with shouldered blocks in order to discharge the loads directly on to
the columns. To arrest any movement of blocks due to their inclined position,
the corner pieces of the pediment extended over two columns and weighed
around 75 tons.

BAALBEK

By a curious coincidence the pediment block of the north-east corner of the Temple of Jupiter has come to lie approximately below its original position on the present temple floor. It is one of the most impressive sculpted pieces of stone in Baalbek, accessible for close inspection by the visitor.

In building it is generally the roof that causes the greatest construction problems. Not only does a large area have to be spanned with as few supports as possible, it has to be made waterproof. In the Greek tradition, the temple always had a saddle roof with a timber frame which carried a suitable roofing material. This could have been burnt clay tiles, slabs of marble or alabaster, or sheets of lead on wooden planks. This last type of roofing was certainly the most expensive but it was also the most durable and allowed full water-proofing at all places. On the outside, the Greeks hid all timber parts behind a stone cladding, but inside the temple the timber construction was fully visible. In their roof design they employed the post and lintel system and consequently the clear span of the timber beams was limited to about 12 m (39 ft), requiring interior supports at this point.

The Romans introduced the truss principle, in which the triangular shape of the roof frame is designed to function as a kind of arch, whereby the main beam at the bottom ties the ends of the rafters together, and intermediate posts and braces connect all parts into a fully integrated structural unit called the truss. The tensile strength of timber makes it a suitable material for the truss, but the carpenter's skill in making the correct interconnections of the various parts is also important. Too little remains of the Temple of Jupiter to enable us to make any reasonable speculation about its roof design, but it is fair to assume that it was similar to the design of its sister temple below. And the Temple of Bacchus is so well preserved that we can obtain a very detailed picture of its roof structure.

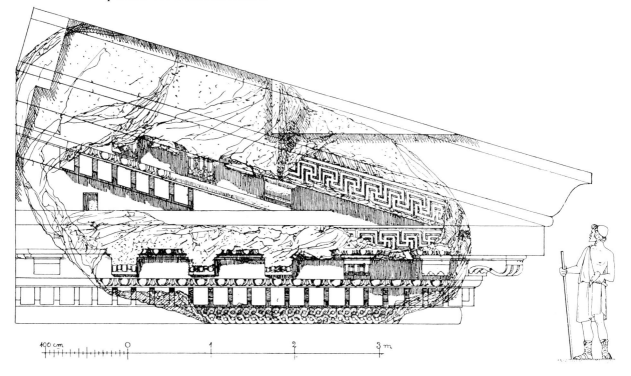

100 cm   0   1   2   3 m

Details of the roof construction of the Temple of Bacchus

One thing is certain: the Romans did not use vaulting to cover the cellas, probably because good cedar wood was still at hand. They certainly disliked the impermanence of wood, its tendency to decay and its liability to burn; but a vault presented great technical problems and was very costly. Let us turn then to the Temple of Bacchus and examine its roof structure. It consists of the ceiling over the peristyle around the temple, and the inner ceiling, over both of which the inclined roof extended.

The external colonnade is covered by huge stone slabs which span the 2·50 m (8 ft) distance between the architrave and the cella wall. These ceiling blocks are each about 5 m (16 ft) long and 1·20 m (4 ft) thick. They average 45 tons in weight each. Their underside is slightly hollowed, and a magnificent geometric lacework of decoration with figurative motifs is carved along their entire length.

The details of roof construction of the interior of the Temple, which has a clear width of 20 m (66 ft), can best be observed on the drawing. We see successive stages of construction.

To the left there is the top of the ceiling slab over the external colonnade. The twenty holes in the upper surface of each block served as anchorage for the lifting devices. They indicate that twenty pulleys were used simultaneously, each lifting 2–5 tons. The grooves in the vertical joints between the blocks provided for the suspension of working platforms for the finishing of the relief.

On the right side we see the upper part of the cella wall with the entablature projecting over the engaged columns. The roof trusses rested on the cella wall and the projecting interior columns; the ends of the beams were dovetailed into the stones and served thus as lateral ties of the whole building. The inclined rafters reached out to the cornice blocks. Various details at the pediment connections suggest that the roofing material consisted of lead sheets which were placed on a layer of boards.

109

Cornerblock of the pediment of the Temple of Jupiter

The skill of the stone masons was extraordinary. They delighted in technical masterpieces and they tended to use large stones, even when these were not structurally necessary. One such example is a block from a stairway tower near the entrance of the Temple of Bacchus. Part of the door frame, projecting steps and a portion of the tower wall are all cut out of one piece.

I said previously that the Romans did not use the technique of vaulting in the temples of Baalbek, but this does not apply to the roof of the Temple of Venus, to the semicircular exedras of the Great Courtyard and the vast substructures below it. The Temple of Venus and the round exedras are covered by domical vaults of precisely cut stones, while the passages below the courtyard are topped by massive barrel vaults. Very wide openings which were to have a horizontal top received a flat arch construction. Probably the most famous example of a flat arch is the lintel over the gate of the Temple of Bacchus, which will be discussed in the following chapter.

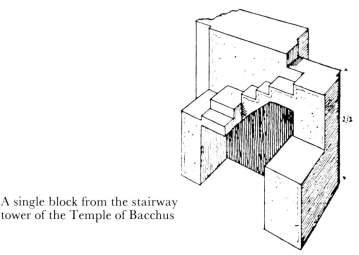

A single block from the stairway tower of the Temple of Bacchus

Organization of the Work

As seen above, the construction of the temples extended over many decades, during which time the traditional sanctuaries were used for worship. Several details indicate that the construction procedure was organized in stages and that different teams of workmen were active at each stage.

There is evidence of a 13 m (43 ft) long access ramp in the southern part of the Great Courtyard which seems to have served for bringing in material during the construction of this portion of the temple without disturbing the northern part. It was later filled in and, as in the rest of the courtyard, the fill contains chips of stones from the dressing of the constructed parts. It is worth mentioning that chips of the red Aswan granite which furnished the material for the column shafts of the courtyard are conspicuously missing. This indicates that these parts had been imported ready made from Egypt.

Several heavy foundations without any apparent structural function seem to have served as bases for lifting towers or derricks. Rough masonry blocks were first brought from the quarries around the town to the construction site where the design was prepared on a flat lay-out surface at full scale. Stones were patterned and cut according to this layout. Before the final erection all stones were fitted together on the floor, to make sure that problems on the scaffolding would be minimized.

What better lay-out surface could there have been than the top of the Trilithon? And indeed, when this portion of the Temple of Jupiter was recently cleared and made accessible to visitors, a large engraved drawing of the pediment was found. It depicts exactly, at full scale, the angle of the raking cornice, the subdivision of the entablature and the position of the modillions. Most probably the drawing was aligned with the actual pediment and served as reference for the positioning of the blocks.

The various parts of a construction were marked by different numbers or letters used by the different teams of masons and contractors to distinguish their work. In the case of the Great Courtyard one contractor using the symbol ⋋⋋ worked on the north side, while the contractor on the south side used the letters MER. Professor Kalayan points out that most of the stones thus marked needed special attention, due either to defects or to their special position within the structure.

On a keystone of the southern subterranean passage next to a bust of Hercules, there is the inscription DIVISIO MOSCHI, suggesting that this portion of the work was done by the Squad of Moschus.

The final dressing of the stones was accomplished by a marginal draft chiselled towards the centre of the surface, exactly delimiting the size of the stone. The rest of the surface was generally dressed with an adze, giving a uniform texture of dents parallel to the sides of the stone. This method was adopted because the mason could face the dressing surface as he worked and cut with regular movements. This is a technique typical of Syria, Lebanon and Palestine, contrasting with the practice of the Greeks who worked most surfaces with chisel and mallet.

Decoration

The decorative details applied last of all with chisels and drills provided the basis for meticulous studies on form comparisons, mainly with the aim of establishing chronological criteria. They confirmed the strong influence of Imperial Rome on the style of decoration in Baalbek without disguising the Eastern influence on planning. A case in point is the position of shell decoration over niches: whereas the key of the shell is always at the bottom in the Orient, Baalbek follows the western-Roman way of putting the key on top.

BAALBEK

Curiously, the lower parts of the buildings were kept rather plain, while lavish ornamentation was spread over the entablature, so high up that details are hard to distinguish. Also, the observer may be struck at first by the endless repetition of unchanging architectural ornamentation on capitals, mouldings and friezes, but a closer look will reveal charming variations made by the individual artist.

There are some lovely and well preserved reliefs on the walls of the water basins in the Great Courtyard, but the masterpiece is the ceiling over the peristyle of the Temple of Bacchus, which constitutes a unique example of classical relief work. Its design is based on a continuous 270 m (886 ft) long geometric ribbon of interlocking pentagons and rhomboids, very much in the Eastern spirit. Floral growth wraps over this quietly flowing pattern within which we barely recognize the badly defaced remains of sixty-six busts. Many of them are thought to depict mythological figures such as Ganymede, Tyche, Ceres, Diana, Minerva, Pluto and others. Some are believed to represent towns in the region, suggesting their financial support of the project. Some of the ceiling blocks are now lying on the ground and can be studied at close range. And examining them and other surviving examples of the meticulous carvings we regret that so much was never finished and that so little was left undamaged.

Cornice detail from the Temple of Jupiter. From the top down, it consists of the gutter moulding with palmette decoration and a lion's head as water spout, followed by twisted bar moulding, meander frieze, consoles, egg-and-dart moulding and dentils (lower left).

Opposite, the peristyle ceiling at the north-east corner of the Temple of Bacchus

The 'Stone of the Pregnant Woman'

Quarrying and Transporting the Stones

There are two quarries near Baalbek which supplied the enormous masses of stone which were needed for the construction of the monuments. One, which is about 1 km ($\frac{1}{2}$ mile) long, is on the northern slope of Sheikh Abdallah hill, on our right as we arrive from Beirut. Being at a higher level than the great temples and at an average distance of only 500 m (1600 ft) from the ruins, this quarry provided all the big blocks which were difficult to transport. Most parts of it are grown over today or serve as a cemetery, but one great showpiece remains: the biggest cut stone in the world, originally destined to continue the Trilithon. Being 21·72 m (72 ft) long and averaging a cross-section of 4·80 by 4·80 m (16 by 16 ft), which translates into a volume of about 500 m³ (650 yds³) and a weight of 1200 tons, the block was never fully separated from its base, and it lies inclined in the quarry where it was cut parallel to a seam in the rock. The block is commonly called Hajar el Hibla or 'Stone of the Pregnant Woman'.

The other quarry is in the middle of the plain, about 2 km (1$\frac{1}{4}$ miles) north of the town. It has remained practically unchanged since Roman times and offers many clues to Roman quarrying techniques.

114

HOW THE TEMPLES WERE BUILT

Normally the blocks were extracted from the face of the natural rock. Vertical grooves were cut around each block from the top down, wide enough to allow space for a man to work. The natural rock being somewhat softer, metal picks were used for this work, and we can see individual blows of up to 10 cm (4 in) in length. After the block was separated on its vertical side, a groove was cut along its outer base and the piece was felled like a tree on to a layer of earth by means of wedging action from behind. It seems that the Romans also employed a sort of quarrying machine. This we can deduce from the pattern of concentric circular blows shown on some blocks. They are bigger than any man could have produced manually, and we can assume that the cutting tool was fixed to an adjustable lever which would hit the block with great force. Swinging radii of up to 4 m (13 ft) have been observed.

When the block of stone had been quarried, the problem of transportation arose. The biggest blocks, such as those of the Trilithon, had their final position close to the ground, and here we may assume that the Romans used the ancient method of 'bury and re-excavate'. This method was widely used by the Egyptians and is a simple application of the inclined plane principle for the moving of great weights. A ramp of compacted earth is brought up to the previous layer of masonry and the next block is pushed and pulled in place over the incline. A block of stone measuring, say, 4 by 4 m (13 by 13 ft) in cross-section and 20 m (66 ft) in length would weigh about 800 tons, and every square centimetre of its base would create a pressure of about 1 kg ($2\frac{1}{4}$ lb) on the ground. In order to move this mass on a well smoothed moist earth surface it would take a force of at least 400 tons to overcome the friction. This obviously was impossible. Therefore, from the earliest times rollers were inserted under heavy loads, often with the addition of a sort of sleigh between the rollers and the weight in order to protect the burden. Many Egyptian and Mesopotamian records of this practice exist. If we assume that the block rested on neatly cut cylindrical timber rollers of 30 cm (12 in) diameter at half-metre distances, each roller would carry 20 tons. If the contact surface of the roller with the ground were 10 cm (4 in) wide, the pressure would be 5 kg/cm² (71 lbs/in²), which requires a solid stone paving on the ramp. The theoretical force necessary to move that block horizontally would be 80 tons. Another possibility is that the whole block was encased in a cylindrical wrapping of timber and iron braces. Vitruvius

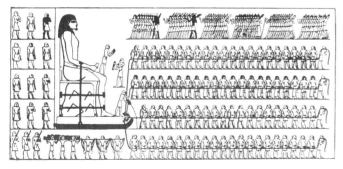

Transportation of a monumental pharaonic statue by means of a sleigh and large pulling crews

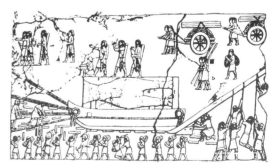

Assyrian relief showing the transportation of a sculpture by means of a sleigh on rollers and a lever

attributes the invention of such a transportation technique to the Greek engineer Chersiphron and his son Metagenes. However in our case the diameter of the resulting cylinder would be about 7 m (23 ft) and the rolling surface would be about 1 m wide, producing a pressure of 4 kg/cm² (57 lbs/in²). The force needed to turn this monstrous load would be somewhat less than 80 tons, but the operation would have been very cumbersome. Also there remains the question of how the block would have been unwrapped and put in place, which brings us to the even more perplexing problem of lifting great weights.

Between A.D. 60 and 70, at the time when the Temple of Jupiter was under construction, Heron of Alexandria wrote the most complete treatise of Antiquity on the theory and practice of mechanics. It is significant that his work has survived only in an Arabic translation by a native of Baalbek called Costa ibn Luka. Ibn Luka produced the translation around A.D. 860 and demonstrates a full understanding of practical mechanics, such as can be taught only by a continuous tradition.

For moving heavy weights Heron recommends the lever as follows:

> The lever was perhaps the first experience of moving exceedingly heavy weights, for people wanting to move great weights found that these first had to be lifted from the ground. Since all the parts of the base of the burden rested on the ground there was a lack of hand-holds. The solution was to dig a little way under it and to insert the end of a long pole under the burden, placing under the pole near the burden itself a stone, properly called fulcrum, then to press down on the other end of the pole, thereby lifting the burden.

Levers were used to adjust the position of stones, to lift them partially from the ground in order to insert rollers and to push them forward, too. But to lift a block right off the ground was not possible with levers.

Yet all the column parts, the entablatures and the peristyle slabs had to be lifted into place as the technique of dowelling requires. The Greeks used to keep protruding knobs on their column drums to be able to attach ropes, or they cut loop-shaped grooves into the vertical faces of blocks for the same purpose. The Romans preferred a more sophisticated device which allowed them to attach the lifting mechanism directly to the top surface: the lewis hole. This is a trapezoidal hole with inclined undercut walls, on an average 20 cm (8 in) long, 8 cm (3 in) wide and 29 cm (11 in) deep. When two metal pieces with inclined sides matching the undercut are inserted with a straight piece filling the space between, the side pieces cannot be pulled out. Heron gives detailed instructions for the choice of iron to be used in lewis holes:

> With this method we must guard against using iron that is too hard, lest it breaks, and we must guard against what is soft, lest it bends and twists under the weight of the stone. But we must use instead that which is in between, neither too hard nor too soft, and it is also

116

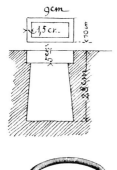

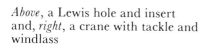

Above, a Lewis hole and insert
and, *right*, a crane with tackle and
windlass

necessary to guard against a bend in the iron or a fold in it, or a crack
that it had when it was made. And the fault in it is serious not only
because the stone may fall, but because it may hit the workers if it
falls.

Due to the good quality of Baalbek stone and the shape of the lewis hole,
which transmits the pulling force practically without bending moment, each
hole can carry approximately 5 tons. The number of holes is determined by the
weight of the block. In heavy stones the holes are usually grouped together at
the necessary minimal distances.

For the actual lifting operation movable cranes or huge and sturdy timber
towers must have been erected, very similar to the practice of reconstruction
work today. The mechanisms used were wheels, pulleys and tackles, with
plenty of rope, activated by capstans or windlasses. Obviously, every part of the
operation, every move had to be carefully planned in advance and the work
had to be rigorously organized. But planning and discipline were basic qualities
of the Romans who demonstrated in Baalbek what magnificent tasks they could
accomplish.

BAALBEK

High Renaissance Rome provides us with a more recent example of architectural weightlifting. This example is relevant because Domenico Fontana, the architect in charge, had the same means at his disposal as the Romans did. Pope Sixtus V wanted the 23 m (75 ft) tall obelisk which Caligula had brought to Rome from Baalbek's namesake in Egypt, put up in front of St. Peter's Basilica. The project included the lowering, transportation and erection of the monument.

Fortunately for us, Fontana was so proud of his achievement that he produced a lavishly illustrated treatise on the job called *Della trasportatione dell'obelisco Vaticano et delle fabriche di nostro Signore Papa Sisto V, fatte dal Cavallier Domenico Fontana, architetto di Sua Santita.*

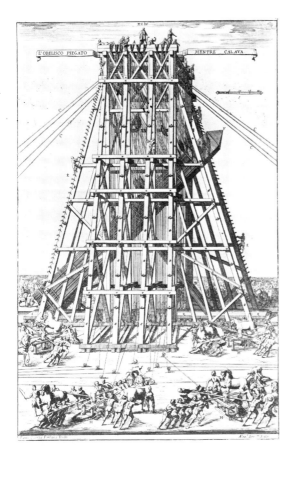

The erection of the Vatican obelisk. It is wrapped in timber tied by wrought iron bands and turns around its centre of gravity causing the base of the obelisk, which is on rollers, to move sideways.

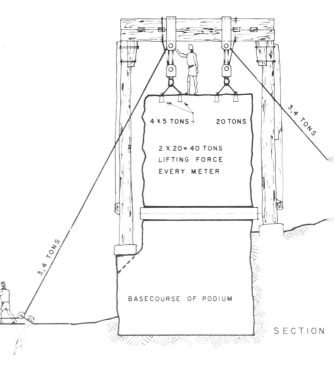

HOW THE TEMPLES WERE BUILT

The preparation of scaffoldings, ramps, and all the necessary gear took seven months. Fontana carefully calculated the weight of the obelisk, which came up to 327 tons, and he decided to use 40 windlasses. The block was encaged in timber and tied with iron rods. The lifting operation required the efforts of 800 men and 140 horses which worked under Fontana's direct command. Trumpets would give the signal to pull and bells would give the signal to stop. Roman operations at Baalbek will not have been much different. The 800 ton block of the Trilithon must have been moved into position by rollers. Then it had to be lifted slightly to allow the removal of the rollers before the tremendous load was lowered inch by inch. If we figure five tons lifting capacity per lewis hole we would need 160 attachments to the stone. Four each could be hooked to a pulley of 20 tons capacity which in the case of six rolls needed an operating power of about $3\frac{1}{2}$ tons. The task therefore consisted of the simultaneous handling of forty windlasses of $3\frac{1}{2}$ tons each. The pulleys were most likely attached to timber frames bridging across the stone.

This feat of transportation was only exceeded in 1775 by Comte Carburi who placed the monolithic base for an equestrian statue of Peter the Great at Leningrad. For this purpose a rough granite block of 1500 tons was moved seven kilometres over land by means of bronze ball bearings. For comparison's sake I give two modern figures: the loading capacity of a heavy duty railroad car does not exceed 250 tons, whereas the take-off weight of the Saturn V rocket is 2800 tons!

Fontana's accomplishment is a brilliant demonstration of the kind of thing that can be done under the leadership of ingenious individuals. The real mystery of Baalbek is the total absence of written records on its construction. Which emperor would not have wanted to share the fame of its creation? Which architect would not have thought of proudly inscribing his name in one of the countless blocks of stone? Yet, nobody lays claim to the temples. It is as if Heliopolitan Jupiter alone takes all the credit.

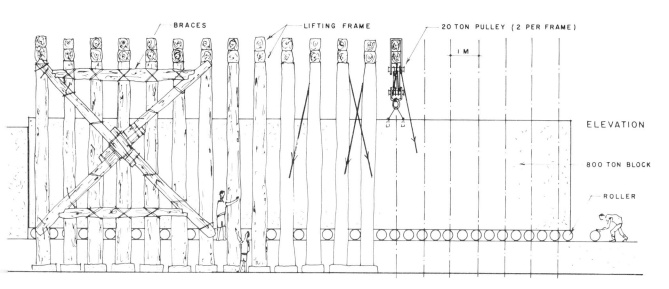

Above, side elevation and, *left*, section of an hypothetical procedure for placing an 800-ton block for the Trilithon

CHAPTER ELEVEN

Restoring and Preserving the Monuments

Having discussed in detail the effort and the skill which went into the erection of the monuments of Baalbek nearly two thousand years ago, we shall now see how modern engineering pays homage to the achievements of the past.

As mentioned in Chapter Nine, many a traveller in the past lamented the ruined state of the buildings, the unchecked devastation wrought by nature and man alike. As time went by and the fortress was abandoned, layer upon layer of rubble accumulated and vegetation started to sprout. People moved in and built their modest houses in the shadow of the mighty temple walls.

Many parts of the ruins were in precarious condition, threatening to fall at any moment, such as the column leaning against the east wall of the Temple of Bacchus, or the top of the gate at the same temple. As we have already noted, the Romans introduced a sort of flat arch and corbel combination to span the 6·33 m (21 ft) wide opening. Surprisingly they added no stepped jointing or other load-reducing device over the opening, relying solely on the buttressing power of the walls to the right and left. No wonder the loss of the roof and the severe earthquakes allowed the enormous pressure of the keystone to take effect until eventually the upper part of the gate was pushed 20 cm (8 in) apart and the 3 m (10 ft) high keystone threatened to drop down completely.

This was a most dramatic situation: few travellers failed to depict it in their illustrations, or at least to give a lengthy account of it. The effect of imminent collapse was given a greater sense of immediacy by the fact that the gateway was buried in debris halfway up, and the onlooker came dangerously close to the suspended block. It was this keystone of the Temple of Bacchus which prompted the first protective action for the antiquities of Baalbek. Around 1870 Richard Burton, the British consul in Damascus, provided an underpinning which was eventually used by the German archaeologists for the lifting of the stone to its original position. The Germans used great winches which they borrowed from French engineers who were then building the railway in the vicinity. The keystone was again tied to the walls by means of an embedded steel beam – and this marks the first reconstructive action taken in Baalbek.

Since then all the temples have not only been protected against further deterioration – today they may even be regarded as earthquake proof – but an extensive programme of reconstruction has been carried out over the years. In order to appreciate fully the scope of the ruins in Baalbek, it is necessary to go

The hanging keystone over the gate of the Temple of Bacchus as seen by David Roberts in 1839

more deeply into the techniques of reconstruction and preservation which I shall present in the following chronological review.

From the beginning, five basic criteria were observed with few exceptions:

1. Reconstruct only those portions which have enough original material to warrant such work.
2. Do not imitate original work when providing necessary replacements but clearly show them as new.
3. Change the original condition of each stone as little as possible in order not to hamper further scientific investigation.
4. Assemble all pieces as faithfully as possible to their original state.
5. Render the whole structure fully resistant to all future destructive forces.

Due to the outbreak of World War I, the German Archaeological Mission had no time to undertake any significant work of consolidation other than that mentioned above. After the War, when Baalbek became part of the French Mandate, the Temple of Venus and the Six Columns of the Temple of Jupiter were among the first monuments to attract the attention of the 'Service des Antiquitiés'. At that time architects F. Anus and P. Coupel were active from the French side, while the Lebanese engineer H. Kalayan took care of the practical execution of the work. Since then Mr. Kalayan, who later became chief engineer for reconstructions of the Lebanese Department of Antiquities and Professor at the American University of Beirut, has been closely associated with the intricate task of reconstruction. Throughout this time we can notice continuous progress in the technology applied.

The building which received most attention was the well preserved Temple of Bacchus. The first task was to insure the stability of the existing remains. The beautiful group of four columns at the south-east corner of the Temple carried an incongruous Arab tower addition, which was removed. The ceiling and entablature blocks were all tied together by reinforced concrete beams; the work can be seen very clearly from the top of the Mamluke tower nearby.

At this time it was discovered that one of the four columns rested on a bearing surface of only 35 cm^2 (5 in^2), a precarious condition which was quickly remedied.

From 1934 onwards, all the nine remaining columns along the north side of the temple were consolidated. It was found that as a result of an earthquake the columns had been pushed out 20 cm (8 in) at the top. Sturdy scaffolds were erected up to the ceiling of the northern colonnade, and with screw jacks each block was lifted sufficiently to let the columns with their entablature return to their original position. The consolidation of this row of columns necessitated also the partial removal of the superstructure. Eventually all frieze and cornice blocks were refitted and tied together with clamps and cement.

In 1935 the final clearing of the temple's interior was accomplished and the pillar-column combination on the right side of the adytum was reconstituted.

Just before World War II the Arab wall in front of the temple was removed to allow a better view of the building. This was the last work completed under the French Mandate. Since then the Lebanese Department of Antiquities under Emir Maurice Chehab has assumed responsibility for the ruins.

After the war the five fallen columns along the west side of the temple were reassembled, an operation which, due to limited means and the magnitude of the task, lasted from 1946 till 1950. Some of the column shafts to be re-erected were relatively undamaged and therefore retained their initial weight of up to 50 tons. As in Roman times, huge timber towers were erected to hold pulleys which were attached to steel cables wrapped around the column shaft. Thus was accomplished the lifting of the heavy load, a task considered not feasible before.

Like the Roman method, the individual column parts were connected with metal dowels, but now a cement grout was substituted for the lead. Over the columns the entablature was re-erected. Dovetail-shaped channels were cut into the top of the architrave blocks to receive a continuous tie beam in reinforced concrete. This had the advantage of an invisible strengthening of the structure. However, it was later observed that temperature changes affected the reinforced concrete more than the stone. As a result fine cracks along the zone of contact were generated, a problem which has been overcome by new methods.

In recent years Professor Kalayan has employed an advanced concept of engineering for the reconstruction of the Lebanese antiquities: the method of 'post-tensioning'. We all know that stone and concrete are very strong in compression but rather weak in tension. If a stone cracks it is usually because one side of it is experiencing too much tension. The idea of post-tensioning is to subject a concrete or stone structure to sufficient permanent compression so that under no condition will tensile forces occur and create cracks. It is similar to a tightly tied package which will not easily rip open.

This method was first used on the Temple of Bacchus in 1961 for the reconstruction of the two freestanding columns at the northeast corner. The columns measuring 17·5 m (54 ft) in height were erected in the usual way but without any connections, being protected by the construction towers. When they were correctly in place the drilling of a hole with a diameter of 10 cm (4 in) in the centre of each column began. Since the available drill was only six metres long the drums of the columns were taken off one by one until the lowest part of the hole was drilled six metres down from the base. Into this hole nine wires each of 7 mm ($\frac{1}{4}$ in) diameter were inserted. They had a cylindrical anchor piece at the end and were secured in place by a cement grout. The wires were of sufficient length to reach up beyond the top of the columns. They were pulled through the hole of each column part, and the complete column was re-erected step by step. Finally a top plate of steel was added to the capital. With hydraulic jacks each wire was subjected to three tons of tension, in which condition the wires were embedded into the column by a fill of liquid cement. Thus the column was put under a compression of 27 tons – or rather tied to the ground by that force – sufficient to secure it against collapsing.

Similar methods are used to equilibrate bulk masonry which has the tendency to lean or to crack, such as the northern anta wall of the Temple of Bacchus. Another application of post-tensioning was in the reconstruction of ceiling slabs covering the peristyle of the Temple of Bacchus. These slabs weigh about 45 tons each. Due to a fall of nearly 20 m (66 ft) they had broken into several pieces. The slabs were assembled and the vertical joints undercut from the top to about two thirds of their height. The corners were bevelled and at the edges 5 cm (2 in) pipes were embedded to protect the stone. Then a 1·5 mm ($\frac{1}{16}$ in) wire was wrapped around each slab, 150 turns being made in three layers of fifty each. Every wire turn was given a tension of 170 kg (375 lb), which added up to a diagonal resultant force of approximately 48 tons. The slab, now fully rigid, was then lifted into position and the joint reinforced with steel and filled with concrete for absolute stability.

The advantage of this method is that the visible surface of the slab is left untouched and that the slab could be consolidated with a mere 15 kg (33 lb) of wire, while with conventional methods hundreds of kilos of steel reinforcement would have been needed. Most recently post-tensioning has been used during the reconstruction of the westside pediment of the Temple.

It is not intended to rebuild the remainder of the exterior colonnade, although most of the pieces of the southern columns still exist, and we may agree that it is more interesting to see the ruined condition of the building on this side. In particular, the famous leaning column is very impressive. That it is a safe leaning column has not only been proven by time but also by scientific calculation.

Immense archaeological treasures must still lie dormant under the present town of Baalbek. The Lebanese Government is now (1980) commissioning a detailed study of the town, and special consideration will be given to the archaeological remains and to future excavation work. This is a welcome initiative, for since the civil war which started in Lebanon in 1975 excavations and restoration work have come to a standstill.

Furthermore the magnificent International Festivals that were held each year at Baalbek have been discontinued for the time being, and the sound and light installations vandalised. Possibly for the first time in history archaeological treasures were taken hostage in an armed conflict: it is said that at one point in the fighting one faction threatened to blow up some of the monuments if its demands were not met. Fortunately, the threat was not carried out, and the mighty ruins seem to witness with unperturbed serenity the troubled times, of which they have seen so many.

SELECT BIBLIOGRAPHY

Alouf, M., *A History of Baalbek*, revised edition, Beirut, 1914

Baumgarten, M., *Peregrinatio in Aegyptum, Arabiam, Palestinam et Syriam*, Nürnberg, 1594

Belon, P., *Les Observations etc.*, Paris, 1553; ed. S. Sauneron, Paris, 1970

Burckhardt, J. L., *Travels in Syria and the Holy Land*, London, 1822

Cassas, L-F., *Voyage pittoresque de la Syrie etc.*, Paris, 1787

Collart, P. and Coupel, P., 'L'autel monumental de Baalbek', *B.A.H.* Vol. LII, Beirut, 1951

Corm, D. (ed.), *Baalbek International Festival Program*, Vols. XIV, XV and XVII (including articles by H. Kalayan, F. Ragette and Z. Zeine), 1969–72

Cumont, F., *Oriental Religions in Roman Paganism*, New York, 1956

Dussaud, R., *Topographie historique de la Syrie antique et médiévale*, Paris, 1927

Harding, G. Lankester, *Baalbek*, Beirut, 1963

Huxley, J., *Man and the Modern World*, London, 1947

Ibn al Qalansi, *The Damascus Chronicles of the Crusades*, trs. H. A. R. Gibb, London, 1932

Jidejian, Nina, *Baalbek: Heliopolis 'City of the Sun'*, Beirut, 1975

Julien, P., *Baalbec*, Beirut, 1870

Kalayan, H., 'Notes on the Heritage of Baalbek and the Beqa'a' in *Cultural Resources in Lebanon*, Beirut, 1969. See also Corm, D.

Krencker, D. and Zschietzschmann, W., *Römische Tempel in Syrien*, Berlin, 1938

Laborde, Léon de, *Voyage de la Syrie*, Paris, 1837

Le Strange, G. (trs.), *Palestine under the Moslems*, London, 1890

Maundrell, H., *A Journey from Aleppo to Jerusalem*, 6th ed., Oxford, 1749

Monconys, B., *Journal des voyages de Monconys*, Lyon, 1665

Pococke, R., *A description of the East and some other countries*, London, 1745

Radzivil, N. C., *Hierosolymitana peregrinatio etc.*, Braunsberg, 1601

Renan, E., *Mission de Phénicie*, Paris, 1864

Roberts, David, *The Holy Land*, London, 1843

Roque, M. de la, *Voyage de Syrie et du Mont Liban*, Paris, 1722

Schaeffer, C., *The Cuneiform Texts of Ras Shamra*, London, 1939

Vitruvius, *The Ten Books of Architecture*, trs. Morris Hicky Morgan, New York, 1960

Volney, C., *Voyage en Egypte et Syrie etc.*, Paris, 1787

Wiegand, Theodor (ed.), *Baalbek. Ergebnisse der Ausgrabungen und Untersuchungen in dem Jahren 1898–1905*, Vols. I, II and III, Berlin and Leipzig, 1921–25 (including contributions by H. Kohl, D. Krencker, Th. von Lüpke, O. Puchstein, O. Reuther, F. Sarre, B. Schulz, G. Schumacher, M. Sobernheim and H. Winnefeld).

Wood, Robert, *The Ruins of Baalbec, otherwise Heliopolis in Coelosyria*, London, 1757

Wright, Thomas (ed.), *Early Travels in Palestine*, London, 1848

And articles and papers by the following:

R. Amy, F. Anus, M. Chehab, C. Clermont-Ganneau, R. Collart, P. Coupel, F. Cumont, M. Dunant, R. Dussaut, L. Jalabert, H. Kalayan, D. Krencker, J. Lauffrey, R. Mouterde, A. Parrot, P. Pedrizet, C. Picard, de Possel, O. Puchstein, S. Reinach, J-P. Rey-Coquais, S. Ronzevalle, R. Saidah, J. Sauvaget, D. Schlumberger, B. Schulz, H. Seyrig, C. Virolleaud, E. Weigand, G. Wiet and others in the following publications: *Berytus, Bibliothèque Archéologique et Historique de l'Institut Français d'Archéologie de Beyrouth, Bulletin du Musée de Beyrouth, Jahrbuch des Archäologischem Instituts, Mélanges de l'Université Saint-Joseph, Revue archéologique, Revue des Etudes Anciennes, Revue Biblique, Syria*, and other journals of learned societies.

Index

INDEX

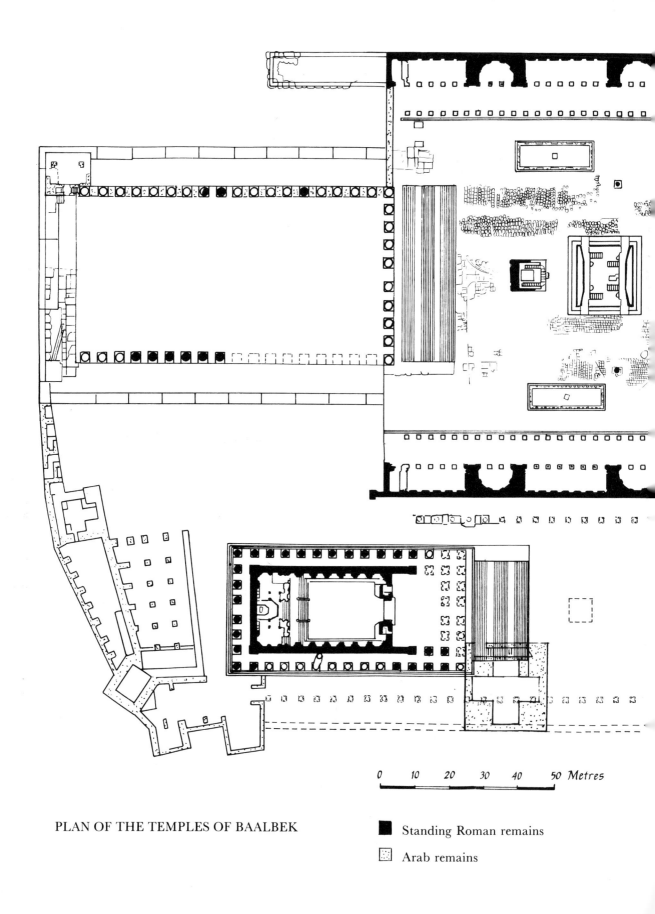

PLAN OF THE TEMPLES OF BAALBEK

0   10   20   30   40   50 Metres

■ Standing Roman remains

▦ Arab remains